FINE WICKER FURNITURE

1870-1930

Tim Scott

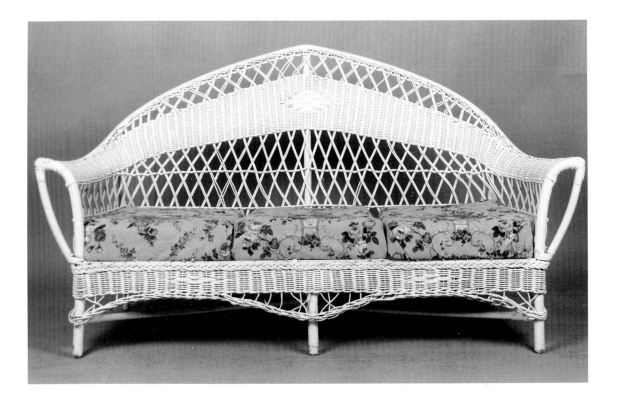

Schiffer Publishing Ltd

1469 Morstein Road, West Chester, Pennsylvania 19380

Acknowledgments

Many thanks to those who allowed us to photograph their collections, including Donny Malone and Harold Swart of Saugerties Auction Services, Joel Zettler of Oley Valley Country Store, Mary Jean McLaughlin of The Summer Place, and Bill Sharon. I am especially thankful to Joel Zettler, who made the price guide for the book possible.

I also thank Lee Ficks of Ficks Reed Company, Dick Hovey of Eastman House, Kathy Flynn of the Peabody Museum, Mark DeFrancesco of H.H. Perkins Company, and Monika Fogarty of William B. Johns & Partners, Ltd., for willing assistance.

Thanks also go to Nancy Schiffer, who greatly assisted in the production of the book, and Robert Biondi, who provided help and humor during the long hours of photographic work.

Title page:
White sofa with arched back, open-weave and closely woven design, and diamond patterns on the back and skirt. Floral cushions with inner springs. Circa 1920s.

Published by Schiffer Publishing, Ltd.
1469 Morstein Road
West Chester, Pennsylvania 19380
Please write for a free catalog.
This book may be purchased from the publisher.
Please include $2.00 postage.
Try your bookstore first.

Contents

Chapter 1
The Roots of Wicker

What is wicker? The word "wicker" is rooted in the Old English *wican* (to give way, collapse); the Danish *vigger* (willow, osier, branch of willow); and the Swedish *vika* (to bend). In modern English it refers to a family of pliant natural and man-made fibers used in the construction of objects--everything from baskets, boxes, floor mats, hats, and shoes, to houses. The flexible nature of wicker has made it especially usable in furniture, and it is in this form that wicker has achieved its greatest popularity. Unlike most furniture made of hardwoods, wicker furniture "gives way" to the body and provides durable, supple comfort.

Wicker furniture has been around almost as long as history has been recorded. Granted, the (barely discernable) wicker chairs seen in relief carvings on ancient Egyptian tombstones do not necessarily match the ornate sophistication of Victorian wicker chairs, but they give evidence that the furniture-making potential of wicker was recognized long ago. Wicker has threaded its way through history. Moses floated down the Nile in wicker thousands of years before Egyptian ruler Menka-Heqet sat on it. King Tut's tomb included wicker chests, baskets, and sandals. Noted Roman historian Pliny wrote of the flexible nature of willow twigs and their use in reclining chairs. Basket chairs became the furnishing of choice for England's peasants in the sixth century. John Donne, Robert Burns, Charles Dickens, and even William Shakespeare mentioned wicker in their works. In *Othello* Act II Scene III, a drunken Cassio threatens, "A knave teach me my duty! I'll beat the knave into a twiggen [wicker] bottle."

TREVES MUSEUM A Toilet Scene with WICKER CHAIR 200 A.D.

Had Cassio seen Harrod's 1910 catalog, he would have had several choices of fine wicker bottles for use in beating the knave.

quart.   quart.   1½-pint.   pint.
No. T U 941.—Oval-shaped Bottles or Flasks. Fitted with patent stoppers. Bottles covered with wicker, in close work, open work, and extra fine close work.

	qt.	1½-pt.	pt.
Close wicker	3/6	3/0	2/6
Open wicker	5/0	4/6	3/6
Extra fine close wicker	6/6	6/0	5/6

Nickel Plated Metal Stoppers, 6d. extra.

Cane Covered Hot Water Tumblers. Most useful Article. Price, 1/4

No. T U 600. Wicker-covered Glasses. Extra Fine Wicker, bound with leather round the top.
Size 1 2 3
1st quality 1/3 1/6 2/0
2nd quality 1/1 1/2 1/3 each.
(To order only).

No. T U 50. Autotherm Vacuum Bottle. Will keep Beverages Hot for 24 hours; complete with Baize lined Basket with Handles; very compact for Travelling. 1 Pint size, Nickel and Leatherette covered, 14/0. Nickel and Leather covered, 18/6; all Nickel, 20/3. 1 Quart size, Nickel and Leatherette covered, 22/6; Nickel and Leather covered, 28/6; all Nickel, 32/0.

No. T U 943. Oval Pocket Flasks, with Patent Stoppers.

	¼	½	1 pt.
Close Wicker	1/6	2/0	2/9
Open Wicker	2/0	2/6	4/0
Extra fine close wicker	3/0	3/6	6/0

In "Elegie I, on Jealosie," John Donne makes reference to the typically English basket chair:

> "Nor when he swolne, and pamper'd with great fare,
> Sits downe, and snorts, cag'd in his basket chaire."

Peregrine White, a baby on board the *Mayflower*, crossed the Atlantic in a wicker cradle. In paintings, plays, and poems, on tombstones and in tombs, wicker has been a part of our environment. We have rocked to sleep in it in infancy and taken it with us to the grave.

The variety of natural fibers known collectively as wicker have roughly similar characteristics and, often, are the products of one plant. However, a brief definition of each of the major materials used in wicker furnishings is helpful.

Raw rattan being prepared for use. The girls are scraping off the knots and bark.

Rattan: This is a type of climbing palm that grows to 600 feet in length that is native to Ceylon, China, India, Malaysia, and other parts of Southeast Asia and the Far East. While there are several hundred species of rattan, *calamus rotang* is considered to be the best for commercial use. The rattan vine has a long stalk (often no more than one and one half inches in diameter) with a thin, hard bark and reversed thorns. In preparing it for export, the rattan is washed with sand, bleached, and dried. The thorny leaves are removed and the vines are cut into sections, leaving the rattan polished and straw-colored, like young bamboo. Vines are cut into lengths, gathered into hanks, and shipped. Rattan can be bent without breaking, and its natural, high-gloss finish and water-resistant strength make it ideal for outdoor furniture. However, rattan does not take stain or paint as well as other wicker materials (although there are a number of painted rattan pieces around). It was the primary material used in wicker furniture until the mid-eighteenth century.

Reed: A by-product of rattan, reed is cut from the central core of rattan after the bark has been removed. Reed came into play in the 1850s and took over from rattan as the most common material used in (what has become) collectible wicker furniture. It is very flexible and porous; can be cut into flat, round or oval shapes; and easily takes stain or paint. Reed derived from rattan should not be confused with grass reeds, which were used much less frequently in wicker furniture manufacture.

Cane: Another by-product of rattan, cane is produced from the bark removed from the rattan plant. Cut into uniform strips for use, cane has the same pliable, high-gloss characteristics of rattan. It often is used for chair seats and backs and as wrapping around the arms and legs of furniture.

Willow: Highly flexible and very versatile, willow comes from willow shrubs and trees. Willow is native to wet lowlands from the Arctic to the West Indies, Central America, Eurasia, South Africa, Madagascar, and areas of Indonesia. Willow often is used in basketry, and came into demand in wicker furniture in the early 1900s. Almost indistinguishable from reed, the blond willow twigs (called *osiers*) have very small knots where the new shoots have been cut off. Osier, almond-leaved, and purple willow are the best varieties for use in furniture making. Willow stains well and is water resistant.

Rush: Derived from the sedge family, rush is a perennial plant with a grasslike stem that rarely is used in wicker furniture. It is classified with other dried grasses such as prairie grass and Oriental sea grass.

Fiber: Known often as fiber-reed, art fiber, and fiber rush, fiber is man-made from machine-twisted paper. Fiber was introduced during World War I by Marshall B. Lloyd, inventor of the Lloyd loom. Soft and flexible, fiber frequently is twisted around thin wire to make it more durable. By 1930 fiber was used in the production of most wicker furniture.

Other materials used in wicker furniture include Oriental sea grass, prairie grass, raffia, and binder cane, although these were used less extensively.

During the 1800s, when a world commerce was achieved by merchant clipper shipping, wicker furniture made the transitions from a common Oriental home fixture, to American and European outdoor furniture, to furniture for every function for every room of the house.

Trade with China was restricted to the port of Canton during the late 1700s. Because of the burgeoning opium trade, Westerners only could do business in trading headquarters known as *hongs*. Here they first set eyes on exotic wicker fantail chairs. Traders brought home samples of these chairs, and the curiosity of Europeans and Americans slowly began to be aroused. However, it was yet many years before wicker furniture was popular with the buying public and the art of making furniture a commercial venture.

Rattan Art Deco armchair with braided edges and cushions. Bottom half of chair (beneath the seat) in hourglass design. Original paint. Circa 1920s.

A porch view of the "Low" House in Shanghai, circa 1890s. The open-weave chairs have woven seats, flat-woven arms, and hourglass bottom design, making them very similar to basket chairs.

After the American Civil War, outdoor wicker furnishings became very fashionable in the growing nation. City dwellers sought summer homes as places to escape from the congestion and increasing pollution of the inner cities. The hygienic value of fresh air and sunshine was recognized, and well-to-do people flocked to the mountains and seashores for rest and rejuvenation. Lightweight, open, weather-resistant, and sanitary, wicker furniture made mostly of rattan and cane became the perfect fit for summer homes. Some painted wicker pieces went indoors to match existing furnishings. Soon, manufacturers realized wicker's adaptability to Victorian styles and designs.

HARRODS Limited, Brompton Road, London, S.W.

BRUSHES AND TURNERY DEPARTMENT.

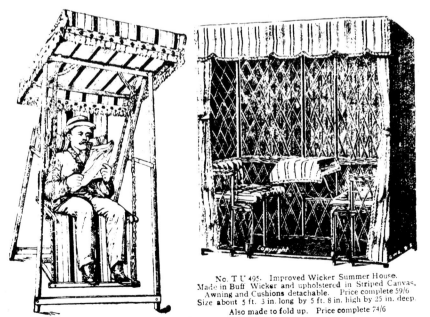

No. T U 12 Swing Hammock Chair. Very comfortable and luxurious, and folds quite flat when not in use. Price 21/0. A cheaper kind can be had, but not recommended.
Willesden Canvas Cover. Price 26/6

No. T U 495. Improved Wicker Summer House. Made in Buff Wicker and upholstered in Striped Canvas, Awning and Cushions detachable. Price complete 59/6 Size about 5 ft. 3 in. long by 5 ft. 8 in. high by 25 in. deep. Also made to fold up. Price complete 74/6

The metamorphosis of wicker furnishings throughout the mid- to late 1800s on into the 1930s is a fascinating and telling parallel to the culture and history of the United States and England. People of the Victorian era were as passionate about their homes as they were reserved and proper in other matters. The Victorian era, in fact the era between the American Civil War and the First World War (1865-1914), was an age of innocence, transformation, and reform. Society was becoming more mobile, women were becoming emancipated, city living was on the rise, international trade was increasing, and the shift from an economic base in agriculture to industry was in full swing. Women were "enticed" by the availability of higher education. All of these changes were perceived as threats to the existing lifestyle. People reacted by redefining the home, making it as warm, attractive, and welcoming as possible and thereby keeping it the center of family life. Enter wicker—exciting, exotic, eye-catching, protean, and one-hundred percent natural.

A proper Victorian woman in 1897.

A: Rolled-arm natural loveseat with beadwork in the sculptured rolls. Restored. Made by Heywood Brothers and Wakefield Rattan Company. Circa 1900s.

B.: Natural Victorian end table with looped edge, stick and ball and curlicue details, wrapped legs, and small woven tier. Natural table lamp in Tiffany style with closely woven design. Table circa 1890s, lamp circa 1910s.

C.: Natural heart-shaped Victorian sewing basket with heart-shaped shelf, close-weave hinged lid, and scrollwork. Circa 1890s.

As society and technology walked hand in hand into the twentieth century, wicker furniture took on a more streamlined, angular, and masculine look. The exotic frills of Victorian wicker were now passé. The rectangular, practical-looking wicker of Austrian and German designers and America's Gustav Stickley grew in popularity during the early twentieth century. Stickley's styles were strongly influenced by the simplicity of Shaker furniture, which was straightforward, functional, and devoid of curves.

As the Lloyd's loom was developed in 1917 and handmade furnishings became more rare, the public slowly began to turn away from wicker. Marshall B. Lloyd was a manufacturer of baby carriages who invented the Lloyd's loom out of necessity. Strikes had plagued his factory in Menominee, Michigan, and Lloyd was struggling to find a way to maintain production and cope with rising labor costs. Invented in the midst of a strike, the Lloyd's loom was capable of machine-weaving wicker furniture from less-expensive man-made fiber—and do the work of thirty men. The loom's trademark was a very tight weave. By 1930, most wicker furniture was made of fiber, much of it manufactured on the Lloyd's loom.

Starting gradually in the 1960s, when a strong popular movement for natural products swept across America, ornate and turn-of-the-century wicker experienced a strong revival in the antiques market. Those who delight in the handmade goods found the enduring strength and charm of this well-made and unique furniture appealing. The superior craftsmanship antique wicker displays by the intricate designs and quality materials has provided many unique furniture forms now well appreciated decades after their execution. The usually unknown men and women who crafted these pieces have left a fascinating variety of forms. Discovering their endless variety is an exciting and satisfying pleasure for many today. No wonder antique wicker furniture is considered a true art form!

A.: Ornate natural armchair from Windsor Chair Company (Nova Scotia). Closely woven seat and back with green details and stick and ball and curlicues on back, arms, and legs. Circa 1890s.

B.: Natural Heywood Brothers and Wakefield Rattan Company (Chicago) armchair and clover-leaf table. Armchair has rolled arms and back with canework in the back and beadwork in the roll on the back. Table has stained oak top, stick and ball and curlicue details along the sides of the top and on the legs. Both pieces circa 1900s.

C.: Matching painted Art Deco armchair and ottoman with floral cushions. Armchair has cutout of leaf pattern on the back; both pieces use closely woven design. Circa 1920s.

Chapter 2

Wicker Furniture's Evolution: 1870-1930

Wicker furniture evolved through many stylistic changes from the 1870s to the 1930s. Early in this period, a strong artistic and romantic reformation rooted in the works of Englishmen Henry Cole, John Ruskin, and William Morris spoke against the increasing industrialization and mass production of furniture. Cole sought an alliance between art and industry; Ruskin wanted industry reshaped so that artistic furnishings instead of bland, cookie-cutter forms could be produced. Morris became the father of England's Arts and Crafts Movement, which sought a return to handcrafts. All three strove for new ideals in what was considered artistic and had a powerful influence on homemakers' tastes. Wicker certainly approached the ideal of artistic, handmade, and comfortable furniture, and began appearing on porches of summer homes in America and Europe.

Ornate: 1870-1890

After wicker firmly established its position on the summer porch, it moved indoors and spread through the parlor, nursery, and bedroom during the second half of the nineteenth century. Manufacturers adapted wicker furniture to elaborate designs with Oriental overtones and the demand grew rapidly. Interestingly, ornate designs first appeared in America; England still seemed content with the basket chair developed during the Middle Ages, with few modifications other than open-plaited skirting. The croquet chair, a larger version of the basket chair, became popular and sold as well as the basket chair through the 1800s.

Green and natural photographer's bench with tight-weave seat, rolled arm, stick and ball and curlicue detail, and leaf motif on the back. Attributed to Heywood Brothers. Circa 1890s.

A.: Natural Victorian settee and armchair from Wakefield Rattan Company. Both pieces have elaborate woven scrollwork and use stick and ball and double twisting throughout. Settee has woven cane back. Excellent pieces. Both circa 1890s.

B.: Natural music stand with stick and ball work, oak shelf, wrapped Aladdin's feet, scrollwork, and hinged sides. Made by Wakefield Rattan Company. Circa 1890s.

C.: Natural Victorian table with oak top, rolled skirt, double twisted balls, and bird cage center structure. Made by Heywood Brothers and Company, Gardner, Mass. Circa 1890s.

HARRODS Limited, Brompton Road, London, S.W.

BRUSHES AND TURNERY DEPARTMENT.
WICKER AND RUSH CHAIRS.

Croquet Chair. Plain Buff Frame.
No. T U 1 ... 3/11   No. T U 3 ... 5/11
2 ... 4/11   „ 4 ... 7/6

No. T U 57.   The "Weybridge"
Chair. Made in Buff Wicker and
Cream Rush.   Price 17/9

No. T U 186.   The "Beaufort" Chair.
Made in Green Rush, 12/9
„ Cream „ 13/9

No. T U 181.   The "Wellington" Chair.
Made in Green Rush.   Price 11/9
„ Cream „ „ 12/9

No. T U 197.   "Selborne" Chair.
Made in Cream Rush and Coloured
Cane. Price 17/9.

No. T U 192.   "Radford" Chair.
Made in Green Rush.   Price 12/9
„ Cream „ 13/9

Child's
"Primrose" Chair.
Buff and Rush.
4/11

Child's
"Princess" Chair.
Buff and Rush.
3/11 4/11 6/6

Child's
"Daisy" Chair.
Buff and Rush.
3/0 3/6

No. T U 208.   The "Catford" Chair.
Made in Cream Rush.   Price 12/9

No. T U 56.   The "Brunswick" Chair.
Made in Buff Wicker and Cream Rush.
Price 17/9

No. T U 55.   The "Molesey"
Chair.   Made in Buff Wicker
and Cream Rush.
17/9

The "Lester." Made in Green Rush. 13/0

A.: Natural rocker with liberty bell motif; serpentine arms, legs, and back with unique weave; cane seat; scrollwork and beadwork; and stick and ball styling. Circa 1890s.

B.: Natural rocker with rolled arms and back, stick and ball work in the back, cane seat, unique weaving set into the roll, and scrollwork on the arms and legs. A beautiful piece. Made by Heywood Brothers. Circa 1895.

C.: Natural Heywood Brothers and Wakefield Rattan Company armchair with green details. Features a cane seat, rolled arms and back, and stick and ball and curlicue details. Circa 1898.

A.: White Victorian rolled arm chaise with continuous and star-caned back plus elaborate scrollwork under the arms and on the wrapped legs. Yellow floral cushions and rolled footrest. The continuous ring and star-caned back make this a very unique piece. Made by Wakefield Rattan Company. Circa 1890s.

C.: Natural high chair with elaborate scrollwork and double twisting. Shelf opens and hooks closed. Attributed to Heywood Brothers and Wakefield Rattan Company. Circa 1898.

B.: Natural baby carriage with wire wheels, rolled hearts on the sides, elaborate scrollwork and stick and ball work. Circa 1880s.

Ornate wicker became the rage in the last twenty-five years of the century. The public loved it, decorators loved it, and the vast number of manufacturers made sure there was no shortage of it. As manufacturers proliferated, set up showrooms, and utilized mail-order catalogs, competition increased and prices went down, making wicker more affordable to the middle class. New wicker designs came into vogue quickly, with companies adapting and changing one another's styles. Wicker's comfort, unlike much of the machine-made furniture that came before and after it, further helped to make it popular. It also was friendly and—most importantly—exotic.

A.: Umbrella basket with curlicues, delicate scrollwork, finials, and ball feet. Made by Heywood Brothers and Wakefield Rattan Company. Circa 1898.

B.: Natural dressing stand in original condition with oak top, beveled mirror, unique spindle, elaborate fancywork, and wrapped legs and mirror supports. Made by Heywood Brothers and Wakefield Rattan Company. Circa 1898.

A.: Natural photographer's chair with double roll, stick and ball and curlicue work, rosettes, and double-twisting. Attributed to Heywood Brothers and Wakefield Rattan Company. Circa 1898.

B. and C.: Unique white-painted Heywood Brothers and Wakefield Rattan Company posing chair with elephant trunk front and Aladdin's feet back. Curlicues all over. A rare piece designed as a photographer's prop. Circa 1898.

Natural etagere with early weave on the shelves, bird cage work, stick and ball work on the top, curlicues throughout, cabriole legs, and lasting charm. Attributed to Heywood Brothers and Wakefield Rattan Company. Circa 1898.

The Oriental mystique surrounding wicker derives from its origin before 1850 as an import from the Far East. The fantail and peacock chairs—with obvious Oriental overtones—steadily proved popular. China and Japan were unknown to the typical Westerner, and hence curiosity about them was strong. Oriental designs had influenced silver, ceramics, and textiles as well.

Japan was opened to the West in 1859. Three years later, at the International Exhibition in London, England, Japanese decorative arts were displayed and were warmly accepted. However, it was another decade before Orientalism and its influence in wicker caught on in America. The 1876 Philadelphia Centennial Exhibition displayed the arts and crafts of fifty-one countries, with the Orientals favorites by far. Close to ten million Americans were exposed to Oriental wares and furnishings—with lots of bamboo—at the exhibition, and shortly thereafter the Oriental style took hold in home decorating. Bamboo and wicker became integral parts of the aesthetic trend in decoration. The studios of many of the artists of the day, among them Robert Blum, James McNeill Whistler, and William Merritt Chase, were furnished with wicker. Needless to say, their acceptance of the style merely reinforced its validity with those interested in arts and things fashionable.

An orgy of styles and influences joined with Orientalism in the 1880s. Byzantine, Elizabethan, Gothic, Grecian, Louis XVI, Moorish, and Renaissance styles often were represented in room furnishings and combined. Victorians found Byzantium and Moorish Spain as exotic as the Orient. Wealthy travelers explored these regions and brought the styles home. Arches and ogees, arabesques, strapwork, diaper patterns, and wildly ornate designs all were found, even in combination, in 1800s wicker furniture. Ribbons, seashells, hand-painted fans, silk flowers, and numerous other accoutrements adorned rooms.

However, Orientalism held sway over the other influences freely used in homes of the day. The arbiters of good taste pronounced the proper ways in which to lay out each room. In 1883 *The Decorator and Furnisher* noted the latest in furnishings, making repeated reference to wicker:

Wicker chairs, which have become such favorites, are now painted in all colors, and when furnished with cushions are exceedingly pleasant to handle and to use. The rattan lounges for a morning room are all the rage. Accompanying footstools are decorated with bright ribbons. Wastebaskets in split bamboo are now decorated with large bunches of artificial flowers tied on with gay ribbons.

Home decorators such as Harriet Spofford, Ella Rodman Church, and others suggested using Oriental draperies and materials, tiles, mats, scrolls, and hanging cabinets with unusual curios. Parasols and fans were recommended for use on ceilings and fireplaces. These items adapted well with wicker, and added a touch of the artistic and an element of the unknown that made a room interesting and exciting.[1]

A.: Rocker with rare shamrock motif, early continuous ring design, cane seat, elaborate fancywork, and caned shamrock. Attributed to Wakefield Rattan Company. Circa 1890s.

B.: Natural rocker with parasol motif featuring rare caning *around* the motif instead of *inside* it. Scrollwork, continuous ring design, and cane seat are additional features. Circa 1890s.

Not all wicker was as elaborate as that previously described. There were variations in late nineteenth-century wicker. While more ornate pieces were rife with flamboyant designs, curves, and frills, the more "sedate" wicker utilized simpler designs, straight lines, and square corners.[2] The more straightforward wicker was less eye-catching, more sober, more harmonious with other styles of furnishing, and more likely to be found in a family room or library. It conformed to the tenets of Charles Locke Eastlake, a reformer in the lineage of Cole, Morris, and Ruskin. Eastlake believed that most furniture should be handmade, comfortable, and without "extravagant contours or unnecessary curves."[3] His views were adapted in designing the less-ornate wicker, although he never personally endorsed wicker furniture.

Whether frilly and flamboyant or more straightforward, wicker of this period exhibited a sensuality and eroticism that seems in contradiction to the Victorian ethos. The Oriental brothel was associated vaguely with ornate wicker furniture, although there is no proof that many actual brothels were furnished with even a stick of wicker. This association very likely comes from wicker's inherent sensuality of form and the notorious "Storyville Portraits," photographs of New Orleans prostitutes and brothels taken around the turn of the century that featured, among other things, wicker furniture. The more streamlined wicker of the day was associated more with the romance novel than the brothel, as its lines were less free-flowing and sensual.

A.: Natural rocker with caned back panel, close-weave seat, serpentine rolled arms, skirt, and back, and elegant scrollwork. Natural square table has oak top, wrapped legs, and abundant scrollwork on the legs and skirt. Small table lamp has open-weave shade with fabric lining. Natural armchair has cane seat, ball feet, rolled arms and back, diamond patterns on the back, and lovely scroll centerpiece in the back. Rocker circa 1890s, table circa 1890s, lamp circa 1900s, and armchair circa 1880s.

B.: Natural child's rocker with shell design in the back and cane seat. Attributed to Wakefield Rattan Company. Circa 1890s.

Turn of the Century: 1890-1910

As the twentieth century approached, ornate wicker was on the wane. The glut of designs and the riotous combinations of styles became vulgar in the eyes of the arbiters of taste. Unfortunately for collectors today, furnishings that had invaded hallways, parlors, dining rooms, offices, and dens were relegated to the attic or summarily discarded.

A.: White recamier with strong Art Nouveau overtones and "Willowware" upholstery. A beautiful and rare piece. Circa 1910s.

B.: White Art Nouveau photographer's chair with fancy leaf pattern on the back, cane seat, and bird cage details on the legs. Made by Heywood Brothers and Wakefield Rattan Company. Circa 1910s.

The turn-of-the-century Art Nouveau movement barely got a passing glance from wicker designers, as the free-flowing, feminine styles and insect and floral forms of Art Nouveau were too similar to ornate Victorian. Although ornate wicker had a very strong connection with Oriental styles (and was losing ground to other designs), Hong Kong club chairs and peacock chairs remained popular well into the twentieth century.

Wicker design largely moved away from the Far Eastern dominance and shifted to Europe and America. Sensual, graceful lines gave way to a more practical, masculine, restrained, and straightforward look. William Morris's influence was felt in German Bauhaus designs and in the Austrian wicker industry, which began in the early 1800s and was subsidized heavily by the Austrian government. Eastlake's design philosophy also was more warmly embraced, and some wicker became downright austere. The angular, straight-lined wicker of the Austrians sacrificed much in the way of comfort. Chairs were made with cushioned seats with innovative floral designs and patterns to improve comfort and make the furniture less stark. Albert and Charles Crampton, of England's Dryad Works, struck a middle ground between the almost dizzying detail of Victorian wicker and the austerity of Austria's product. Dryad's wicker was made of willow and featured broad arms with flaring, full-length skirts and well-rounded backs. The Cramptons' designs found a ready audience in America, which loved the style and was impressed by the sturdy, nail-and-tack-free construction.

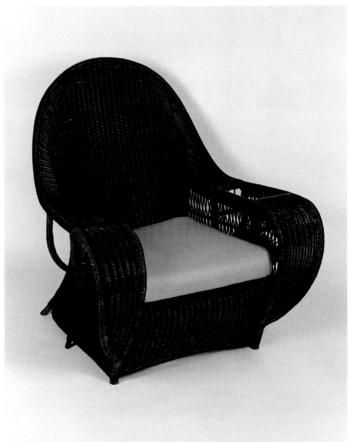

B.: Natural Dryad Works (England) armchair with black diamond pattern on the back and one cushion. Closely woven design with magazine pocket and drink holder on the arms. Circa 1915.

A.: A fine tight-weave Dryad armchair with flat woven arms, woven seat, and open-weave design in the back. Circa 1910s.

A.: Platform rocker with Mission-style overtones and tightly woven back and seat. Extra-large floor lamp with silk-lined open-weave shade. Rocker circa 1880s, lamp circa 1910s.

B.: Dark green rattan couch in the Mission style with cushions. Part of a set including a lounge and chair. Circa 1910s.

At the same time, America found a native son whose wicker designs made a powerful impression. Gustav Stickley developed what became known as the Craftsman or Mission style, which featured wicker echoing themes of the Arts and Crafts Movement in England and American Shaker furniture. With rectangular, almost square shapes; close weaving; and squared-off backs and arms; Stickley's ruggedly masculine style was a complete rebellion against ornate design. Mission-style wicker (the term derived from the sturdy, clean-lined furnishings of Southwest American Franciscan missions) enjoyed great acceptance from the early 1900s to around 1920. Americans escaped to the country for health and recreation in greater numbers, and Mission wicker supplanted earlier wicker as the style echoing the rustic, homey, natural themes of the day. As wicker furniture became more of a fixture in resorts and hotels, country clubs, and summer homes in the mountains and at the shore, it took on names to match the resorts. Bar Harbor, Cape Cod, Newport, and Southhampton designs came into vogue. These styles combined Dryad, Mission, and other

The Prince George and Tampa Bay hotels both featured Bar Harbor-style open-weave wicker furnishings in their lounges and tea rooms. Circa 1910s.

SUN PARLOR KILAUEA VOLCANO HOUSE

A.: Mission-style close-weave armchairs with close-weave backs in the Sun Room of Honolulu's Volcano House. Circa 1915-1925.

design elements and shared the limelight with Mission-style wicker. Upholstery was by now an integral part of these designs. Bar Harbor furnishings differed in their open-weave design, a practical reaction to the ever-increasing cost of labor. An open-wéave Bar Harbor chair took much less time to make than a close-weave chair of any style. Cape Cod designs were closely woven and utilized reed.

B.: White very rare six-legged armchair with serpentine arms and back in Bar Harbor style. With blue cushions and ball feet. Circa 1910s.

DRYAD CANE

A FEW OF THE PLACES WHERE DRYAD FURNITURE
HAS BEEN SUPPLIED

A. and B.: Dryad chairs aboard
a cruise ship and an airplane.

C.: Fancy open-weave arm-
chairs with upholstered seats
aboard the Maynard and
Hudson. Circa 1920s.

INTERIOR OF FIRST VICKERS VIMY PASSENGER AEROPLANE
When Commercial Aeroplanes were started the Dryad Works made the design for
the first Aeroplane Chair, also the pattern now in use

INTERIOR PARLOR CAR, CONCORD, MAYNARD & HUDSON ST. RY. CO.

By the first decade of the twentieth century, virtually *everything* was being made from wicker. Oil lamps; baby carriages; bird cages; planters; airplane seats; railroad seats; chairs with woven side pockets for magazines, beverages, and books; and phonograph cabinets all were manufactured in wicker versions. Practicality was an important factor in airplane seats: wicker was the lightest and strongest material usable. Perhaps one of wicker's greatest moments was as the airplane seat that carried Charles Lindbergh across the Atlantic in *The Spirit of St. Louis* in 1927. Wicker's anti-resonant characteristics made it well-suited in phonograph cabinets. Advertisements for floor and table models stressed the advantages over wooden cabinets and the purity of tone. Wicker's sanitary qualities made it perfect for baby carriages.

A.: Natural finish Victrola in tight-weave design, with cabinet for extra music and star-caning above door. Circa 1920s.

B.: Natural baby carriage with close-weave design and wire wheels and suspension. Natural Lloyd's loom baby carriage with diamond patterns on the side, wooden wheels with rubber tires, and windows in the hood. Left carriage circa 1910s, Lloyd's loom carriage circa 1920s.

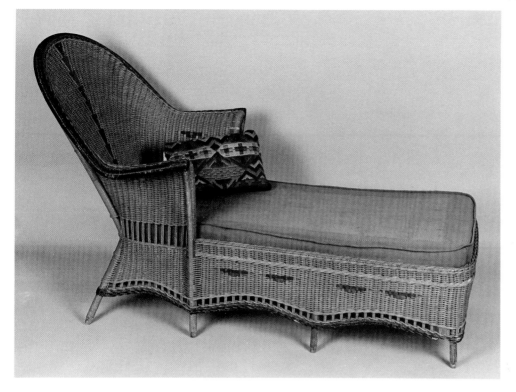

A.: Natural Art Deco chaise lounge with green and red patterns in the back and on the sides. Close-weave design. Circa 1920s.

Art Deco design principles were incorporated into wicker furnishings during the 1920s, yielding gently flowing lines and motifs such as the diamond pattern. The diamond pattern (seen in earlier designs but more prevalent in the 1920s) was woven into the backs of chairs, settees, and sofas and painted different colors to make it stand out. Upholstery and inner springs for extra flexibility and comfort were characteristic. Dining room sets and sets of chairs became popular, as did library tables and davenports. Almost all Art Deco wicker was machine

B.: Dining room set. Oval extension table has two extension leaves and ten matching chairs. Circa 1910s. China cabinet in natural, green, and orange from Heywood Brothers and Wakefield company.

A.: Brown lectern with rolled edge and brass reading lamp. Tightly woven design with a shelf and diamond pattern on front. Circa 1910s.

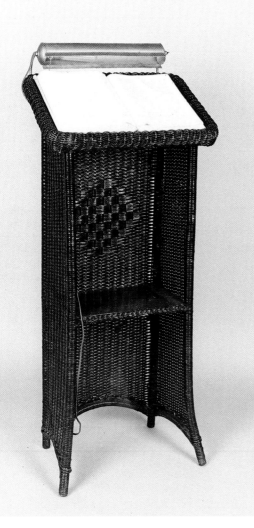

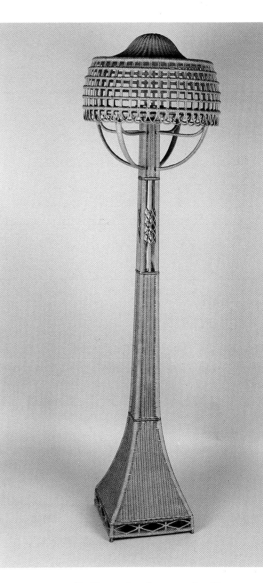

B.: Natural and orange Art Deco floor lamp with close-weave design, scrollwork on the column, and very unique shade. Circa 1910s.

made. The last frontier for wicker—the kitchen was "settled" when wicker buffets and china cabinets were introduced. Porch swings took wicker back outdoors. Radio cabinets, "Eiffel Tower" lamps, coat racks, tea carts, smoking stands, and primitive "Lomodi" hide-a-beds made the Art Deco period a time when one could completely fill a house with wicker furniture. Sea grass and prairie grass were used more frequently. These materials cost more than man-made fiber and could not be machine-woven, but they gave the piece the unique charm of a handmade product. Painted wicker was more common; bold greens, blues, and reds were popular, although white, black, and forest green remained the standard colors. New techniques in enameling were developed and applied as well.

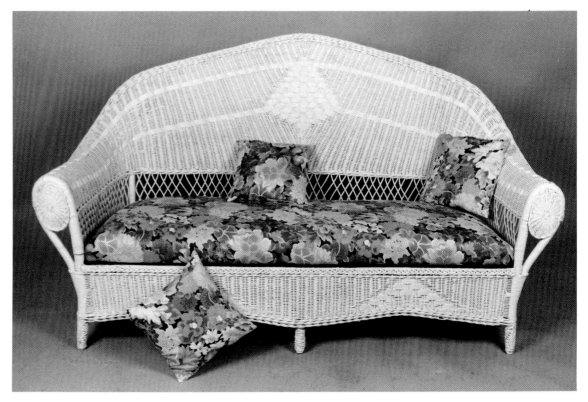

A.: White sofa with one-piece floral cushion and three pillows. Closely woven design with triangles in backrest and on skirt. Wrapped legs and rolled armrests. Circa 1920s.

B.: Green sofa and chair with red and black diamond patterns in the back and floral cushions. Tight weave design. Circa 1920s.

A.: Matching white rocker and armchair with floral cushions and pillow, serpentine arms and back, diamond patterns on the backs and skirts, and overall close-weave design. Circa 1920s.

B.: Orange sofa with white cushions and pillows and diamond patterns in back and large skirt. Closely woven design. Circa 1920s.

A.: Natural table with oak top and matching natural armchairs with floral cushions with inner springs. Table has one wooden shelf. Armchairs have tightly woven design, rolled arms, and multicolored diamond patterns on the back. Table circa 1910-1930, armchairs circa 1920s.

B.: Matching dark green rocker and armchair with brown floral cushions, close-weave design, and diamond patterns on the backs. Circa 1910s.

Decline

Wicker's popularity suffered a precipitous decline in the 1930s. By then the qualities that first had made wicker so fashionable—hand manufacturing, comfort, and natural materials—were gone. Wicker after World War I was mass-produced and machine made of inferior materials and man-made fiber. There were wicker furnishings to fill every nook and cranny of the house. The public had overdosed on wicker.

One indication of wicker's fall is seen when comparing the Fort Dearborn Watch and Clock Company's catalogs for 1923-1924 and 1931. The 1923-1924 catalog devotes twenty-one pages to wicker furniture, with two of those pages featuring furnishings made of fiber. The 1931 catalog has just five pages showing wicker furniture, the vast majority of it made of fiber.

Some have singled out the Lloyd's loom as the cause of wicker's demise, but the glut of uniform, mass-produced Art Deco pieces played a role as well. Other materials now were available for home furnishings, including plastic, chrome, and wrought iron, and they dug into wicker's market as well. Wicker still was produced throughout the 1930s, but the market was shrinking and manufacturers had run out of new designs with which to tempt the public. They tried increased advertising, heavier upholstery, and handmade pieces (with a machine-made appearance) but to no avail.

When wicker's glory days were over, many manufacturers closed down. Wicker's resurgence in popularity since the 1960s has been largely confined to the antiques market, where Victorian, turn of the century, and early twentieth-century pieces have brought good prices.

Much of the wicker furniture made today uses Oriental-inspired designs; some manufacturers create new styles, others make reproductions of classic pieces.

Notes

[1] Kathryn Boyd Menz, *Wicker in the American Home* (Newark, Del.: University of Delaware, 1976), p. 15.

[2] *Ibid.*, pp. 10-11.

[3] *Ibid.*, p. 24.

An example of the agony and the ecstasy of wicker: a beautiful natural platform rocker and a rather mundane painted desk from the last days of wicker's glory.

A.: Natural platform rocker with rolled serpentine arms and back, star-caned back panel, cane seat, scrollwork on the back, and loops beneath and arms and seat. Orange desk with wooden top and close-weave design. Rocker circa 1880s, desk circa 1920s.

B.: White close-weave desk with gallery, wooden top, wrapped legs, and one drawer. White chair with close-weave design. Both pieces circa 1920s.

One Hundred Years

For 100 years Heywood-Wakefield has been building fine furniture. The new reed and fibre suites and single pieces now on display represent the achievement of this century of experience. With their smart designs, vogue upholsteries, and luxurious comfort, they stand apart from the commonplace.

HEYWOOD-WAKEFIELD COMPANY

Executive offices. Boston, Mass.
Six Factories and Eleven Warehouses in the United States
Canadian Factory: Orillia, Ontario

Baby Carriages, Windsor Chairs, and Door Mats are also manufactured by this 100 year old company.

Heywood-Wakefield
REG. U.S. PAT. OFF.

Chapter 3

Wicker Furniture Manufacturers

Dryad

From the American Civil War until 1930, when wicker furniture was in its heyday, well over one hundred companies in the United States and Europe were involved in manufacturing and/or importing these furnishings. While some of these companies faded quickly after the public abandoned wicker in the 1930s, several others had been incorporated into the Heywood-Wakefield Company, which became the largest wicker furniture maker in the world. Some companies retooled to make different products, and others, such as Bielecky Brothers of New York City, continued to make wicker furniture by hand.

Notable English wicker manufacturers from the 1860s through the early twentieth century included Dryad Works, Maple and Company, and Slocombe and Son. Maple and Company, with showrooms in London, Paris, and Buenos Aires, had an enormous catalog of furnishings, including an abundant selection of wicker. Like other English manufacturers, they had a broad international market. Slocombe and Son, established in the 1860s, grew their own willow.

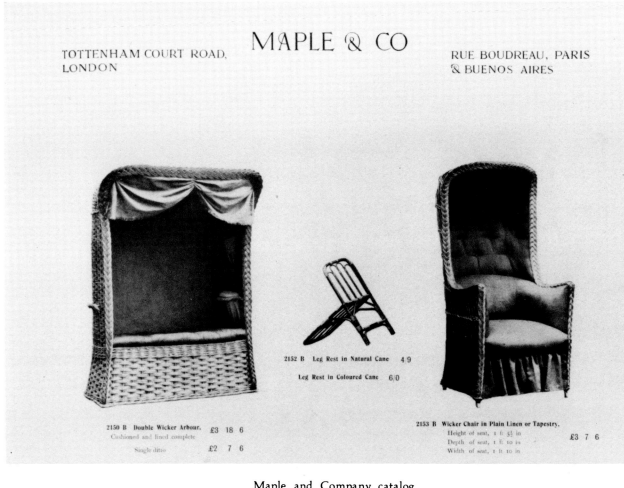

Maple and Company catalog page. Circa 1910.

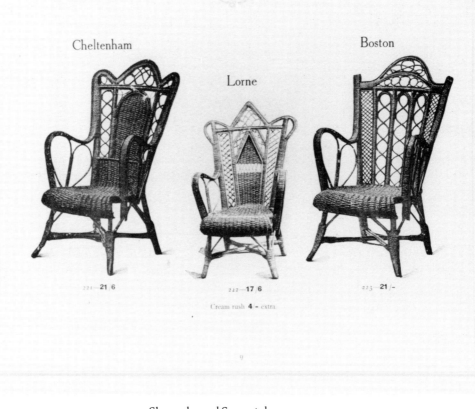

Slocombe and Son catalog page.
Circa 1914.

Their 1914 catalog shows a wide range of upholstered Bar Harbor pieces as well as other styles. In addition to developing styles that became very popular in America in the early twentieth century, Dryad Works was unique in its chair design. Constructed of hardwoods and cane—with no nails or tacks—their chair frames were "built like a bridge" and "shaped for comfort." Dryad used a very tight weave, using more cane and thus providing a heavier chair. Airlines, shipping lines, railways, hotels, hospitals, and even golf clubs were among Dryad's clientele.

Finer points of Dryad Works chair construction, featuring the tight weave and wrapped stakes. From the Dryad Works catalog. Circa 1928.

NO. 298. FLOWER STAND. £8.15.0
Total height 36½ in., width 38 in., depth 17 in.
With three painted metal trays.

NO. 4410. SCREEN. £5.5.0
Total height 60 in., 18 in. panels.
LINED SILK
LINED CRETONNE ... £4.0.0
UNLINED £2.15.0

A.: A page from Dryad Works catalog. Circa 1928.

B.: Natural two-tiered multi-sectioned planter with tight-weave design, braidwork on the skirt, and ball feet. Made by Dryad Works (England). Circa 1915.

Karpen
FURNITURE

Decorative, informal, inexpensive, and truly American

An Indian squaw sat before her wigwam. Her bronze fingers wove deftly, swiftly. A basket of curious beauty grew, strand upon strand, while her papoose played at her side. Centuries later, her primitive art was to be reflected in what an eminent decorator, after careful consideration, has designated as "the only truly American furniture."

Lovely among examples of this native furniture is the *Carrollton*—latest of *Karpen handwoven fiber* designs. In its ebony, Indian-motifs of Navaho red and green are set like brilliant jewels. Summer lives perpetually in the flowered cretonne of its yielding, sagless Karpenesque cushions. There is gracious ease in every graceful line, and staunch strength in its seasoned hardwood frames and steel-cored, vertical fiber strands.

Add its other characteristics: its low price, its long life, its lightness; and one readily understands why the vogue for handwoven fiber pieces grows daily—for living rooms, clubs, and rest rooms, as well as for porches and sunrooms. But in choosing it, as in buying upholstered furniture, there is only one way to be certain of famed Karpen quality. Look for the Karpen nameplate before you buy.

The name of the dealer who can supply you with the *Carrollton* group, and our absorbing booklet of good furniture, *The Glorious Adventure of Home Furnishing*, will be gladly sent to you. Just mail the coupon below to S. Karpen & Bros., 801 South Wabash Avenue, Chicago; 37th and Broadway, New York; or 180 New Montgomery Street, San Francisco.

ASK FOR KARPEN FURNITURE · · FIND THE NAMEPLATE BEFORE YOU BUY

J. and C. Berrian

Before 1870 J. and C. Berrian of New York was one of the largest manufacturers of wicker furniture. Writer Gervase Wheeler noted in 1851 that Berrian had the most extensive catalog of wicker at that time, including armchairs, children's swings, cribs, fire screens, foot benches, rocking chairs, and sofas. Berrian is said to have employed several thousand workers during the 1850s. Their creativity with wicker is to be applauded, their range of products was quite broad.

Ficks Reed Company

The Ficks Reed Company of Cincinnati, Ohio, began making rattan and wicker furnishings in 1885. In its infancy, the company manufactured woven reed and wicker baby carriages under the National Carriage and Reed Company name. As wicker evolved and its popularity expanded, Ficks and Reed moved in step. The company's wicker manufacturing peaked in the 1920s, and as wicker faded in the 1930s Ficks and Reed moved into the production of rattan furniture. Rattan has been the mainstay of their business from the 1930s until today, and they still produce fine furnishings.

Natural rattan sofa (ninety-four inches long) with plump cushioning and bow-tie-on back cushions.

Chittenden and Eastman Company

The physical necessity for a Midwest distribution point for wicker and other furnishings brought Chittenden and Eastman into existence in 1865. Through solid leadership and insightful planning, Chittenden and Eastman grew to become the largest supplier of furniture in the Midwest in the late eighteenth century. Their 1875 catalog featured items as diverse as children's carriages, cabinet hardware, undertaker's trimmings, mouldings, stains, and glass plates. A substantial portion of their business was in wicker furniture, including chairs, sofas, carriages, tables, ferneries, and so forth. Although they primarily were suppliers and not manufacturers of wicker furniture, they played a large role in spreading wicker westward. Chittenden and Eastman evolved into Eastman House, which today produces fine wood furniture.

Edition October, 1916.   A–211   Square Brand

CHITTENDEN & EASTMAN COMPANY, BURLINGTON, IOWA.

No. 270—Reed Foot Stool.
Brown Finish.
Top 11 x 17 in. Height 10 in.
Weight 4 lbs.

No. 488—Reed Fern Stand.
Brown Finish.
No. 1488—Reed Fern Stand.
Old Ivory Finish.

Height 54 in. Weight 12 lbs.

No. 476—Reed Magazine Stand.
Brown Finish.
Quarter Sawed Oak Top 16 x 16 in.
Shelves 12 x 12 in. Height 30 in.
Weight 10 lbs.

No. 455—Reed Flower Stand. Brown Finish.
No. 1455—Reed Flower Stand. Old Ivory Finish.
Size 11 x 28 in. Height 32 in.
Removable Metal Pan. Weight 15 lbs.

No. 1676—Reed Tea Wagon. Brown Finish. Removable Tray
with glass bottom lined with cretonne. Height 29 in.
Tray 16 x 22 in. Weight 15 lbs.

An armchair and sofa from Bielecky Brothers' vintage collection. Both pieces feature hand-woven reed on a rattan frame with decorative braid-work around and under the knee. Diamond pattern designs are in green, charcoal gray, and natural finish.

Bielecky Brothers

The original Bielecky Brothers, Andrew and Conrad, emigrated from Galicia in southern Poland—a willow-weaving region—around the end of the nineteenth century and set up shop in New York's lower East Side in 1907. They began making willow basket chairs with openwork stick wicker and curved backs. They carried their products on their backs, and peddled them on the streets of New York City. Orders were taken from nearby residents; a comfortable and expertly made chair cost $1.50. As business increased, they hired five Polish weavers and added new styles to their production line. Today Bielecky Brothers has an extensive catalog (well over one hundred pieces) of wicker furniture, including a vintage collection with reproductions of pieces from wicker's halcyon days. Prices have gone up a bit, but the excellent, handmade quality remains.

The Best Gift of All

Whether she be bride or matron, young or old, every woman appreciates any article which enhances the attractiveness of the home; if at the same time the gift is a useful one its value is doubled. The best gift of all for bride, wife, mother, or anyone else dear to you is

Heywood-Wakefield
TRADE MARK

Reed and Rattan Furniture

It is attractive, light, sanitary, durable and comfortable. It combines maximum strength with minimum weight. It can be easily cleaned and easily moved. It can be used in any room.

This furniture is especially adapted for use in summer homes. It imparts an air of coolness and comfort.

Style 78120

The rattan of which it is made is the finest grade grown in the Malay Jungles. Our own representatives make selections for us and ship them direct to our ware rooms. These rattans are split into the long, smooth and pliable reeds and are then woven by hand into the designs shown in our catalogues.

We can finish this furniture in any shade, to harmonize with other furnishings. Those pieces enameled in white or the delicate colors, with gold leaf trimmings, are most decorative and at the same time are quite as serviceable as those less pretentious. They are ideal as gifts.

Ask the dealer to show you the newest patterns in this popular furniture. Insist on seeing the little white tag ☞ Heywood-Wakefield It is the guarantee of superior workmanship, material and durability. Accept no substitute, but write at once to our nearest warehouse, giving the name of the dealer you would prefer to patronize and we will tell you how to order through him. Let us know which of these catalogues interests you and we will forward it by return mail.

Style 7854-A

Style 7858-D

Book F, Reed and Rattan Furniture   Book 6, Go-Carts and Baby Carriages

HEYWOOD BROTHERS and WAKEFIELD COMPANY

New York   Boston   Buffalo   Philadelphia   Baltimore   Chicago   San Francisco   Los Angeles   Portland, Ore.
Agents for London and Liverpool, England, J. C. PLIMPTON & CO.

Several companies in Austria and Germany took advantage of the American public's lessening infatuation with Victorian styles at the turn of the century. Conservative, angular designs and Bauhaus-influenced styles became popular, and later were supplanted by Dryad's furnishings.

The most-storied and well-known manufacturer was the Heywood Brothers and Wakefield Rattan Company. The company's history is long and involves several other companies that were incorporated into Heywood-Wakefield over several decades. Heywood-Wakefield's history also involves two major manufacturers—Heywood Brothers and Company and Wakefield Rattan Company—which consolidated in 1897. These two companies were in direct competition for many years, and their development has many interesting parallels.

WAKEFIELD CLIPPER SHIP "HOOGLY"
DISCHARGING A CARGO OF
RATTANS
AT CONSTITUTION WHARF,
BOSTON.

Wakefield Rattan Company

The founding of the Wakefield Rattan Company has a certain undeniable drama.

One morning in the year 1844 a young man stood on a wharf in Boston watching the unloading of a vessel just arrived in port. A stevedore threw a small bundle of rattan over the railing of the ship. The moment for which the youth was waiting had evidently arrived and [he] hastened up to the mate and asked what he intended to do with the discarded rattan. He was told that it was of little value and served chiefly as ballast to prevent the cargo from shifting on its long voyage from the East. So he secured the rattan for a small sum....[1]

The young man with the keen interest in dunnage was Cyrus Wakefield, a partner with his brother in a grocery store who had come to Boston to seek his fortune. On that day at the dock, Wakefield's ship very literally had come in. Wakefield began to experiment with the material, using it to wrap chair legs. He turned his first purchase of rattan over to basket makers, who stripped the reed for weaving. The outside covering of the rattan was sold to chair makers, who used it for chair seats. Seeing the positive financial aspects to dealing in dunnage, Cyrus Wakefield sold his share of the grocery business to his brother and began his jobbing trade in rattan.

Cyrus Wakefield was concerned with the slow and laborious task of stripping cane from the reed, a difficult job that only could be done by hand. But Wakefield had a friend in the business—his brother-in-law, who was with a company in Canton, China. Wakefield arranged to have the cane stripped in China and shipped to America, which saved a great deal of time and labor costs, and led to an increasing supply of the material. Within a few years he hired ships to bring what once was considered dunnage—and now was precious cargo—to America.

The Wakefield Rattan Company began with two crude machines and a few small buildings in what was then South Reading, Massachusetts (South Reading later was renamed Wakefield in honor of the man who had contributed a town hall and so much to the town's industry). The primary early products were all varieties of baskets and hoops for hoopskirts. Because of Wakefield's resourcefulness and his development of new machines, he employed roughly two hundred workers and was far outproducing his chief rival, the American Rattan Company, within ten years. Early wicker furnishings produced by Wakefield's company combined rattan, cane, and willow.

When China's Tái-píng Rebellion temporarily cut off the flow of rattan in the 1850s, Wakefield and his right-hand man, Scotsman William Houston, devised a procedure for spinning shavings into "yarn" to make floor coverings and mats. Houston had acquired knowledge of spinning and weaving in Scotland, and his experience led him to weave the first brush mat of rattan. Houston's ingenuity and Wakefield's concern with wasting materials led them to use all parts of the rattan—cane, reed, and shavings. In 1876 Houston developed Kurrachee rugs, which were popular for many years.[2] He also is credited with the production of rattan window shades and table mats and the invention of a loom capable of weaving chair seats. Soon railroad and trolley cars featured seats with cane webbing devised by Houston. Wakefield began using reed, earlier used for hoops in hoop skirts, in the production of wicker furniture.

As the demand for wicker in general and Victorian wicker in particular increased, so did Wakefield's production. By the 1870s, Wakefield's factories and warehouses covered ten acres of floor space. However, at the height of success, tragedy was not far away. Wakefield incorporated the Wakefield Rattan Company during the financial crash known as the Panic of 1873, and died, bankrupt, of a heart attack two weeks later. The company was reorganized. Nephew and namesake Cyrus Wakefield II returned from Singapore, where he acted as the company's representative, and took control of the foundering business. Prosperity returned within a few years, and the Wakefield Rattan Company regained its strong position in the industry. Wakefield expanded to the West Coast, and at the 1876 Philadelphia Centennial Exhibition received an award for "original design and superior workmanship in furniture, chairs, and baskets of an otherwise waste material...." They also were cited for their cool, clean, and comfortable car seats. By 1879 Wakefield had sold over two million dollars worth of rattan furniture. This is an extraordinary figure when you consider that the average chair cost between two and eight dollars at the time. Even more significantly, this shows the sheer demand for wicker—especially when you consider that there were more than seventy companies manufacturing wicker at the time. Wakefield's catalogs during the 1880s featured goods priced from two to seventeen dollars, including a wide assortment of children's furniture, book stands, couches, divans, footstools, lounges, ottomans, piano stools, stands, and more than seventy varieties of rocking chairs. Designs were rife with stars, fans, hearts, sailor's knots, palms, and sunbursts. Pieces could be ordered bronzed, stained, shellacked, or painted.

Shortly before his death in 1873, Cyrus Wakefield began supplying Levi Heywood with rattan. By the 1870s Heywood Brothers and Company was the largest wooden chair manufacturer in the United States, with bentwood and Windsor chairs their chief products.

A.: Natural Wakefield Rattan Company revolving piano stool with cane seat and back detail, stick and ball work on the back, and ornate scrollwork on the back and legs. Circa 1890s.

B.: Natural music stand with scrollwork, stick and beadwork, wrapped legs, and oak shelf. All original. Attributed to Wakefield Rattan Company. Circa 1890s.

B.: Natural platform rocker with cattails done in double twisting, elegant fancywork, and cane seat. Made by Wakefield Rattan Company. Circa 1890s.

A.: Natural early corner whatnot using unstripped rattan and featuring quatrefoils and curls. Attributed to Wakefield Rattan Company. Circa 1880s.

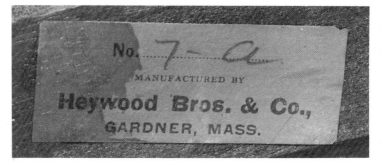

Heywood Brothers and Company

Heywood Brothers and Company began in a little shed next to their father's farmhouse in 1826. The Heywood Brothers chair company grew steadily, with a warehouse in Boston in 1831 and a new manufacturing plant at Crystal Lake in 1834. Levi Heywood, the driving force of the Heywood Brothers enterprises, was an inventive genius who developed machines for making chairs with wooden seats and a wood-bending process that strongly impressed Vienna's Francis Thonet, then the head of the world's largest chair manufacturing company. Heywood also was a pioneer of sorts who simply pushed his way through obstacles. As he watched a fire destroy his factory buildings in 1862, he said, "If the good Lord lets me live ten years, I will make some money yet."[3] He lived twenty years more and did. Heywood's keen sense of humor also is noteworthy.

His impatience with employees who watched the clock was well known. He was greatly disturbed, during one period, because the machinists habitually washed up early so that they would be ready to leave the moment the whistle blew. He already had reprimanded them several times with his usual austerity. One day, five minutes before closing time, he found the men lined up with their coats on ready to dash from the machine shop with the blast of the whistle. Everyone expected an angry outburst, for the old gentleman glared when he came upon them, but he waited a moment and then drawled: "I'm going to play a hell of a trick on you men one of these days. I'm going to tell the engineer to blow the whistle ten minutes ahead of time."[4]

By the 1870s Heywood had invented a machine that could split and shave rattan, another of his fine creations to simplify woodworking and natural fiber processing.

A.: White extra-large whatnot in early design with curved wooden shelves edged in rattan, ornate scrollwork and lattice-work along the top, and oval patterns in the back. Made by Heywood Brothers. Circa 1885-1890.

B.: Victorian natural Heywood Brothers armchair with cane seat, elaborate fancywork, closely woven rolled arms, bird cage design on legs, scrollwork, and stick and ball detail. Circa 1890s.

Oak and bentwood rocker with replaced seat webbing, crest rail with pressed design, and wicker scrollwork. Made by Heywood and Morrill Rattan Company (Chicago). Circa 1890s.

Heywood also had his own version of the ingenious William Houston in A. Watkins. With power looms that wove cane into continuous sheets to his credit, Watkins went on to develop an automatic channeling machine. This device cut a furrow around wooden chair seats so that sheet cane could be pressed into the furrow and secured with a triangular-shaped reed, a "spline." The use of sheet cane now became widespread. New experiments by Heywood allowed rattan to be bent even more, and the increased design possibilities yielded more dramatic, fantastic results.

In the 1880s competition between Wakefield Rattan Company and Heywood Brothers and Company, the titans of American wicker, became intense. "Both firms grew at about the same rate, both were being managed by first or second generations, and both were making related products...."[5] The friendly but competitive rivalry continued, and provided "an outstanding example of how competition helps to stimulate inventiveness, improves product value, lowers prices, and in general makes business better all around...."[6] The rivalry came to a head around 1883, when both companies were attempting to secure a Chicago factory and warehouse.

In spite of their competing interests, they decided to establish a joint manufacturing enterprise there. Representatives of both firms met in Chicago for the purpose of finding a suitable building. The first day's search was fruitless, so it was decided to renew the quest the following day. The next morning, however, the Wakefield men left early, found a plant and informed the Heywood representatives that the building was so satisfactory that they would purchase it independently and operate it themselves.[7]

Needless to say, this did not go over well with the Heywood Brothers representatives. However, they found a suitable plant in the not-too-distant future. No doubt competition became even more intense after Wakefield's sleight of hand.

Heywood Brothers and Wakefield Rattan Company

In 1897 the two titans consolidated. Wakefield Rattan Company had started with a bundle of dunnage, Heywood Brothers began production in a shed. The two had grown to become the chief wicker furniture manufacturers in the United States. Combined, Heywood Brothers and Wakefield Rattan Company was the world's largest importer of rattan and the largest manufacturer of chairs, baby carriages, mats and matting, and an assortment of other cane and reed products. Many today consider Heywood-Wakefield's crowning achievement the phonograph cabinets for the "Perfek'tone Reproducer," which yielded better sound reproduction thanks to wicker's anti-resonant qualities, and was, stylistically, among the best designed wicker furnishings made.

THE HEYWOOD-WAKEFIELD COMPANY

W.B. Washburn Company, Erving, 1848

Walter, Levi, Seth, William, & Benjamin Heywood Chairmakers, Gardner, 1826

American Rattan Company, Fitchburg

B.F. Heywood & Company Partnership, 1835

Washburn Heywood Chair Company, 1905

Gibbs Chair Company, Kankakee, Illinois

Heywood & Wood Partnership, 1844

Levi Heywood & Company Partnership, 1849

Cyrus Wakefield, Rattan Jobber, 1844

Heywood Chair Manufacturing Company, Joint Stock Association, 1851

Wakefield Rattan Company, Incorporated, 1873

Heywood Brothers & Company, 1861

W.R. Company, Purchased A.R. Company, 1875

H.B. & Company, Purchased ½ Stock W.B.W. Company, 1870

W.R. Company, Purchased G.C. Company, 1893

Heywood Brothers & Wakefield Company Consolidation, 1897

Oregon Chair Company, Incorporated, 1906

H.B. & W. Company, Purchased Other ½ W.H. Chair Company 1916

Lloyd Manufacturing Company, Menominee, 1906

H.B. & W. Company, Purchased O.C. Company, 1920

H.W. Company, Purchased Lloyd Manufacturing Co.–1921 Heywood-Wakefield Co.–1921

A.: Large natural Victorian rocker with rolled arms and back, cane seat, and very elegant fancywork. A magnificent piece. Made by Heywood Brothers and Wakefield Rattan Company. White ottoman has ball legs, circular woven design, and open-weave work and bead-work on the sides. Rocker circa 1890s, ottoman circa 1880s.

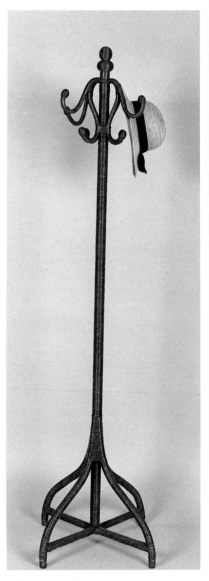

B.: Natural and green photographer's bench with cane seat, rolled arm, and stick and ball and curlicue detail. Made by Heywood Brothers and Wakefield Rattan Company. Circa 1898.

C.: Natural coat rack wrapped completely in cane. A rare piece. Made by Heywood Brothers and Wakefield Rattan Company. Circa 1898.

A.: Matching natural Victorian rocker and armchair from Heywood Brothers and Wakefield Rattan Company. Both pieces have elaborate beadwork and scrollwork on the heart-shaped back and legs, cane seats, and a great deal of character. Circa 1880s.

B.: White Morris chair with blue cushions from Heywood Brothers and Wakefield Rattan Company. Rolled arms with stick and ball, curlicues, and wonderful detail. Adjustable back. Circa 1898.

Cost considerations led to the development in 1904 of a machine that spun twisted paper from wood pulp. The resultant product, fiber, was as pliable as any natural wicker material and more resistant to breaking. It was inexpensive (thus making a close-weave chair less costly) and retained any shape imaginable with glue. Fiber's only drawback was that it was not water-resistant. Regardless of fiber's qualities, various species of willow—American green, Lemley, and purple—were increasing used in the newest designs. Successful experiments were conducted with prairie grass and Oriental sea grass. Manufacturers still preferred these raw materials to fiber.

A.: Black and natural Tiffany style floor lamp with wicker finial, close-weave design and single-bulb fixture. Attributed to Heywood Brothers and Wakefield Rattan Company. Circa 1915.

B.: Rocker with stick and ball and curlicue work, rolled serpentine arms and back with beadwork in the back, star caning in the back, cane seat, and lots of charm. Made by Heywood Brothers and Wakefield Rattan Company (Chicago). Circa 1900s.

Lloyd Manufacturing Company

Marshall B. Lloyd, head of the Lloyd Manufacturing Company, invented the Lloyd's loom in 1917 and effectively cornered the market on machine-made baby carriages. The Lloyd Manufacturing Company was consolidated into the newly renamed Heywood-Wakefield Company in 1921. Lloyd's incorporation into Heywood-Wakefield made the largest company even larger, and gave Heywood-Wakefield the lion's share of the then-booming baby carriage business.

At their height of business in the 1920s, Heywood-Wakefield had seven factories, thirteen warehouses, over 5300 employees, and more than 4.3 million

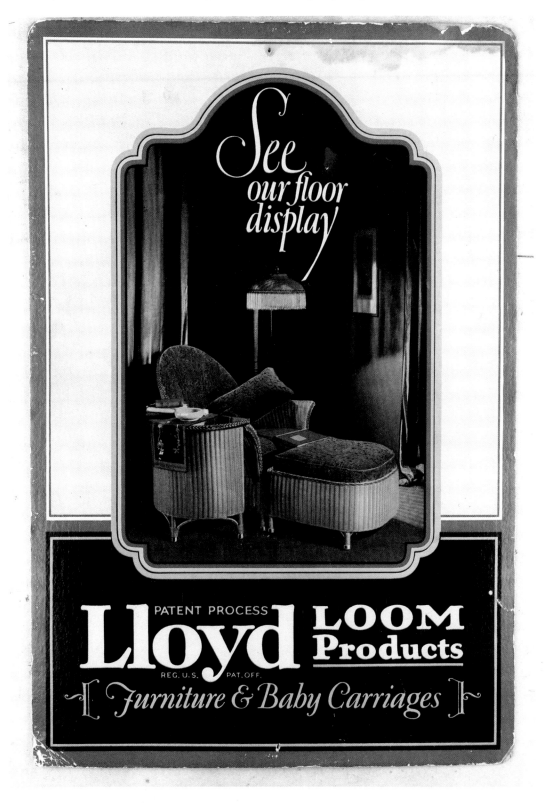

See our floor display

PATENT PROCESS
Lloyd LOOM Products
REG. U.S.   PAT. OFF.
Furniture & Baby Carriages

feet of floor space. Manufacturers that had been incorporated into Heywood Brothers and Company and Wakefield Rattan Company over the years include the W.B. Washburn-Heywood Chair Company (1916), American Rattan Company (1875), Gibbs Chair Company (1893), Oregon Chair Company (1920), and Lloyd Manufacturing Company (1921).

Although this amalgam of various wicker furniture manufacturers clearly was the largest, other companies had a share in sales during the turn of the century. Gendron Iron Wheel Company of Toledo, Ohio; Joseph P. McHugh and Company and Minnet and Company of New York City; Prairie Grass Furniture Company of Glendale, New York; Charles Schober Company, Bloch Go-Cart Company, and John Wanamaker Company of Philadelphia, among others, were successful in importing and manufacturing wicker furnishings. Gustav Stickley was a notch above many of the others in terms of design and scope.

Gustav Stickley

Stickley's oak and wicker furniture premiered at a trade show in Grand Rapids, Michigan, in 1900. His sedate, masculine wicker styles became popular, and his philosophy on furnishings was presented in *The Craftsman*, a monthly publication. Stickley's grasp extended to the home-building industry. He built a bungalow,

Generously proportioned natural rattan lounge chair with plump cushions and bow-tie-on back cushion. Square ottoman (thirty inches) and bunch table (twenty-one inches) are part of the set from Ficks Reed.

furnished completely with his Craftsman furniture, in Morris Plains, New Jersey. The Craftsman Building opened in New York City in 1905—furniture, home plans, metalwork, textiles, pottery, rugs, and art were on display in this twelve-floor vision of the larger-than-life Stickley. Unfortunately, a petition of bankruptcy was filed against The Craftsman, Inc., in 1915. Inexpensive imitations of his designs and a revival of American Colonial styles, as well as his overextension in business, brought Stickley's short-lived business empire down.

By the 1930s the Great Depression had effected businesses worldwide, and the public lost interest in wicker. Many wicker-manufacturing companies fell by the wayside while some of the larger companies retooled and moved into different furniture forms or different industries. Heywood-Wakefield made wooden and school furniture; Bielecky continued to make wicker furnishings. Bielecky's flexibility in allowing decorators to modify their furnishings, originate new designs, and order from old catalogs has helped them continue.

Wicker's halcyon days were over, but the plethora of styles and the unique charm of sturdy, handmade, one-of-a-kind pieces lives on in antique wicker from the 1870s to the 1930s. The greatest era of the art form may have passed, but the art itself lives on.

Notes

[1] *A Completed Century, The Story of the Heywood-Wakefield Company, 1826-1926* (Boston: The Heywood-Wakefield Company, 1926), p. 12.

[2] *Ibid.*, p. 16.

[3] Richard N. Greenwood, *The Five Heywood Brothers: A Brief History of the Heywood-Wakefield Company During 125 Years* (New York: The Newcomen Society in North America, 1951), p. 15.

[4] *Ibid.*, pp. 14-15.

[5] *Ibid.*, p. 17.

[6] *Ibid.*, p. 17.

[7] *Ibid.*, pp. 17-18.

Graceful natural rattan baker's rack (forty-three inches wide by eighty-one inches high) with double verticals, woven cane, and glass shelves.

A.: Natural Victorian side chair with rolled back, elaborate scrollwork on the back and legs, and cane seat. Chair has red label of Heywood Brothers and Wakefield Rattan Company, Gardner, Mass. White sewing basket has hinged lid; open-weave design; fancy scrollwork on the handle, top, sides, and legs; and woven bottom shelf. Both pieces circa 1880s.

C.: White sewing basket with hinged lid, closely woven design, and woven bottom shelf. Basket has red label of Heywood Brothers and Wakefield Rattan Company, Gardner, Mass. Natural ornate side chair with cane seat, elegant scrollwork on the back and wrapped legs, and harp-shaped design on the back with diamond pattern. Sewing basket circa 1920s, side chair circa 1880s.

B.: Ornate white side chair with cane seat and back panel, elaborate scrollwork and beadwork on the back and legs, circles with scrolls on the back, cathedral back supports, and wrapped legs. White sewing basket with handle, fancywork all over and bird cage design on the support. White rocker with green cushion, serpentine arms and back, cane seat (under the cushion), and open-weave design. Side chair circa 1880s, sewing basket circa 1880s, and rocker circa 1910s.

Chapter 4

Seating

Chairs

1880s

A.: Natural Victorian chair with elaborate scrollwork on the back and legs, red velvet cushion and backrest, and bird cage features on the back and legs. Three-legged two-tiered natural smoking stand by Heywood-Wakefield. Natural sewing table with hinged lid has scrollwork on the wrapped legs and diamond pattern on the side most visible. Chair circa 1880s, smoking stand circa 1900-1920, sewing table circa 1910s.

B.: Natural rocker with cane seat, rolled arms and back, star-caned back panel, and lovely scrollwork. Oval table has wooden top, open-weave skirt, wrapped legs, and ball feet. Rocker circa 1880s, table circa 1910s.

A.: White ornate armchair with elaborate scrollwork and bead-work on the back, arms, and legs, and closely woven design. A very unique piece. Circa 1880-1900.

B.: White ornate side chair with round woven seat, wrapped legs and back, elaborate scrollwork and fancywork on the legs and back, bird cage design on the back supports, and twisted reed columns on the back. Circa 1880-1900.

C.: White armchair with rolled serpentine arms and back, curlicues and beadwork on the back, and ball work on the feet. Circa 1880s.

1890s

A.: Natural tea cart with woven top tray and shelves, wrapped legs, and wooden spoke wheels. Natural settee with serpentine arms and back, cane seat under cushion, and elaborate scrollwork on the back and legs. Natural photographer's chair with serpentine arms and back, cane seat, very detailed scrollwork on the arms and beneath the seat, and tight-weave design on the back with a diamond pattern. Tea cart circa 1910s, settee circa 1880s, photographer's chair circa 1890s.

B.: Yellow corner chair with fancy scrollwork and stick and ball work on the back and legs and bird cage work on the arm supports and legs. White table with woven top and fancywork around the top and bottom shelf and on the legs. Ornate white side chair with elaborate fancywork and scrollwork on the back and legs, cane seat, and close-weave design and diamond pattern on the back. Corner chair circa 1890s, table circa 1890s, and side chair circa 1880s.

C.: Unique Victorian natural armchair with rolled arms, scrolled back, mushroom seat, scrollwork beneath the seat, and beadwork on the back. Natural ornate tea cart with removable tray and woven bottom shelf. Armchair circa 1880s from Heywood Brothers and Company. Tea cart late 1890s from Heywood Brothers and Wakefield Rattan Company.

A.: Planter in black wicker frame, red armchair with white cushion, and white ornate platform rocker with rolled arms and back. Planter has elaborate scrollwork on the legs and supports and metal plant holder with flowers on its exterior. Red armchair has open-weave design and stick and ball work on arms, back, and legs, and an overall shape similar to Mission furniture. Rocker on right combines close-weave and open-weave design with elaborate scrollwork and circles under the arms. Planter circa 1890-1910, armchair circa 1900-1915, and platform rocker circa 1890s.

B.: White circular table has wooden top and shelf with braidwork around the edges. White armchair features cane seat, rolled serpentine arms and back, stick and ball work on the back, and elaborate scrollwork on the back and legs. Table circa 1920s, armchair circa 1890s.

C.: White armchair with rolled arms and back, closely woven seat, scrollwork on the legs and back, and abundant stick and ball work. Table has wooden top and two shelves and open-weave design. Armchair circa 1890s, table circa 1910s.

A.: White armchair has serpentine rolled arms and back, cane seat, ball legs, and inverted triangles in the close-weave back and side sections. White oval table has wooden top, braidwork along the side, open skirting, and wrapped legs. Armchair circa 1890s, table circa 1910s.

C.: White banjo and harp motif chair with early design of continuous ring and hand-caned banjo. Painted cane seat. Circa 1890s.

B.: Oak Morris chair frame with elaborate scrollwork on the flat arms, skirt, sides and back, and wrapped arms and legs. Circa 1890-1910.

A.: White ornate armchair with woven seat, elegant scrollwork and fancywork on the back and legs, rolled back, ball feet, and finely detailed round pattern on the back. White end table with woven top and shelf with scrollwork and ballwork. White armchair with floral cushion, ball feet, unique back design, and Mission style appearance. Left armchair circa 1880s, end table circa 1900-1920, right armchair circa 1900-1915.

1900s

B.: Natural armchair with rolled serpentine arms and back, open-weave back, cane seat, and ball feet. Natural square table has oak top, bird cage center support, wrapped legs, and elaborate fancywork on the legs. Table lamp has open-weave shade and silk fringe. Armchair circa 1900s, table circa 1900s, and lamp circa 1910s.

C.: Ornate white rocker with cane seat, elaborate scrollwork on the back, arms, and legs, and rectangular close-weave work on the back. White small table with opening top has six legs and close-weave design. White armchair has ball legs; cane seats; and serpentine arms, back, and legs. Rocker circa 1880s, table circa 1900s, armchair circa 1920s.

A.: Natural Victorian side chair with serpentine back, elegant scrollwork on the back and skirt, balls on the wrapped legs, and tight-weave design with oval open-weave work on the back. Natural towel stand with woven base and wrapped column. White corner chair with tightly woven seat and open-weave skirt and back. Side chair circa 1890s, towel rack circa 1900-1920, corner chair circa 1910s.

B.: Green magazine rack with scrollwork and wrapped legs. Natural rocker with serpentine arms and back, tight-weave design, diamond pattern on the back, and green cushion on a cane seat. Unique natural boat-shaped sewing basket with hinged lid, scrollwork on the legs and supports, oak shelf, and close-weave design. Magazine rack circa 1910s, rocker circa 1900s, and sewing basket circa 1890s.

C.: Bamboo side chair with cane seat. Rattan table with wooden top and shelf. Both circa 1900-1920.

1910s

A.: Matching white Bar Harbor armchair and rocker with patterned cushions and backrests, close-weave serpentine arms and backs, and ball feet on the armchair. Circa 1910s.

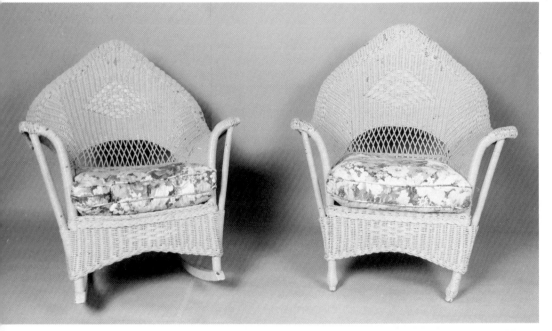

B.: Matching yellow rocker and armchair with floral cushions, diamond patterns on the arched backs and skirts, open-weave work in the lower backs, and close-weave design overall. Circa 1910s.

C.: White oval table with wooden top and tight-weave skirt. White armchair has serpentine rolled arms and back, fabric seat, and open-weave design. Table circa 1920s, armchair circa 1910s.

A.: Natural sewing box/seat with hinged lid, fabric on back-rest and lid, green diamond pattern on the front, and red trim. Natural desk has wooden top, woven shelf, and wrapped legs. Matching chair has cane seat, wrapped legs, and close-weave back. Sewing box/seat circa 1920s, desk and chair circa 1910s.

B.: Matching white arm-chair and rocker with unique open-weave design, floral cushions, serpentine braided arms and backs, and ball feet on the armchair. Circa 1910s.

C.: Natural armchair with rolled arms and back, cane seat, ball front feet, and open-weave design. Natural desk has gallery wooden top, ball feet, and wrapped legs. Armchair circa 1910s, desk circa 1900s.

A.: Gold chair with fancy scroll-work on the back and wrapped legs, cane seat, ropelike wrapping on the back, and a tightly woven strip running vertically up the back. Black lamp with silk-lined open-weave shade. Orange sewing table with tight-weave design, ball feet, and bottom shelf. Chair circa 1890s, lamp circa 1910s, sewing table circa 1920s.

B.: White Bar Harbor armchair with balls on the feet and a cane seat. White desk with wrapped feet, wooden top and drawers. Armchair circa 1910s, desk circa 1920s.

A.: White Bar Harbor armchair (part of a set of four) with cushion and white ornate armchair with cane seat and back panel and elaborate scrollwork on the back and legs. Bar Harbor armchair circa 1910s, ornate armchair circa 1890s.

B.: White Lloyd's loom square table with wooden top and shelf and close-weave sides. White lamp has close-weave design. White rocker has close-weave design, floral cushion, diamond pattern on the back, and unique flat woven arms. All pieces circa 1910s.

C.: Green chest for four drawers in close-weave design. White rattan armchair with orange trim and orange cushion and backrest. Half-round natural end table with oak top, tight-weave work, and wrapped legs. Chest circa 1920s, chair circa 1910s, and table circa 1910s.

A.: White rocker with long skirt, stick and ball work, loops under the arms, and unusual back. Large white plant stand with close-weave design widening into an open-weave top. White Bar Harbor rocker with inner-spring cushion that has almost Mission-style lines. Left rocker circa 1910-1930, plant stand circa 1910s, and Bar Harbor rocker circa 1910s.

Opposite page:

B.: White Bar Harbor rocker and armchair and table with stained oak top. Rocker and armchair have serpentine arms and back and floral cushions. Table has wrapped legs with latticework and wrapped supports. Rocker and armchair circa 1910s, table circa 1920s.

B.: Unique cathedral back armchair with tight-weave design, diamond pattern on the back, and ball feet. Circa 1900-1920.

A.: White armchair with closely woven design and diamond patterns on the back and long skirt, white rocker with both open-weave and tight-weave design, and white armchair with open-weave and tight-weave design. Armchair on left has wrapped legs, reed circles in the arms, and floral cushion. Rocker has wingback styling and floral cushion. Armchair on right has floral cushion with inner springs and diamond patterns on the back and skirt. Armchair on left circa 1920s, rocker circa 1910s, armchair on right circa 1910s.

C.: White armchair with open-weave pattern on the back, woven flat arms, close-weave design, green cushion, and long skirt. White round table with woven open tray top and shelf and ballwork on the feet. Unique white armchair with round seat, open-weave design, ballwork, patterned cushion, and green trim. Left armchair circa 1910s, table circa 1910s, right armchair circa 1900-1920.

A.: White Bar Harbor armchair with flat woven arms, wingback shape, ball front feet, and floral cushion. White planter has circular woven top and wrapped legs. Rattan planter has woven green top and elongated hour-glass-type design. Armchair circa 1920s, white planter circa 1910s, right planter circa 1910-1930.

B.: White Bar Harbor style armchair and rocker, both with patterned cushions and back-rests. Both employ open-weave and tight-weave design in the backs and arms. Circa 1915.

1920s

A.: Natural oval table, armchair, and planter. Table has oak top, woven shelf, and wooden supports with ball feet. Armchair has tightly woven design, diamond patterns on the back and skirt, and a cushion with inner springs. Planter has tightly woven design and wrapped legs. Table circa 1910-1930, armchair circa 1920s, and planter circa 1920s.

B.: Matching white rocker and armchair with floral cushions, large rolled arms, ball feet (armchair), and unique patterns woven into the backs and skirts. White table with wooden top and wrapped legs. All pieces circa 1920s.

C.: Matching orange armchair, rocker, and oval table. All pieces have diamond patterns and closely woven design. Rocker and armchair have open-weave work by the arms, large skirts, and white cushions. Circa 1920s.

A.: Natural finish side chair and armchair. Side chair has tightly woven design, lengthy skirt, wrapped legs, and a unique pattern on the back. Armchair has tightly woven design, wrapped legs, floral cushion, inner springs under the seat, and upholstery across the back. Armchair is part of a set including an extra-large sofa. Side chair circa 1900s, armchair circa 1920s.

B.: Natural wingback reed rocker with cushion and floral back upholstery. Log carrier with circular woven base. Bar Harbor armchair with uniquely woven arms. Rocker circa 1920s, log carrier circa 1900-1930, armchair circa 1910s.

A.: Natural side chair with cane seat, ball ears, and scrollwork on the back. Natural kidney-shaped desk has wooden top, drawer, and wrapped legs. Side chair circa 1890s, desk circa 1920s.

B.: Dark green desk with matching chair. Desk has wooden top and gallery. Chair has a cane seat. Floor reading lamp features brasswork and silk fringe on the shade. Desk and chair circa 1920s, lamp circa 1910s.

C.: White fiber armchair with cushion and ball front feet. White table with circular woven top and metal legs. Armchair circa 1920s, table circa 1930s.

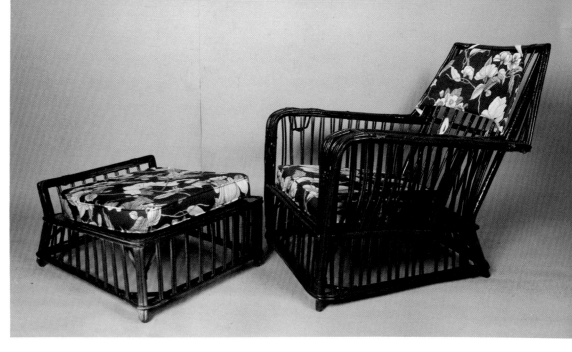

B.: Tall white fernery. White chair has close-weave design, with diamond pattern on the back and wrapped legs. Desk has wooden top and drawer, gallery, and wicker frame. Fernery circa 1920s, chair circa 1910s, and desk circa 1920s.

A.: Green rattan armchair and matching ottoman with floral cushions and backrest. Drink holder in arm. Circa 1920s.

C.: White desk with wooden top. Matching white chair with woven seat. Table lamp has fabric-lined open-weave shade. Desk and chair circa 1920s, lamp circa 1910s.

A.: Rattan Art Deco armchair with cushion, table, and lamp with original paint (orange and green). Lamp has original silk fringe. Armchair has hourglass design beneath the seat. Circa 1920s (all three pieces).

B.: Two natural armchairs. Left armchair has colorful diamond pattern on the back, ball front feet, tightly woven design, green and natural open-weave work on the back and arms, and floral cushion with inner springs. Right armchair has balls on legs, rolled arms and back, a cane seat under the cushion, and Bar Harbor open-weave design. Left armchair circa 1920s, right armchair circa 1910s.

Rockers

1870s

C.: Rocker with cane seat, American flag motif in the back featuring star caning, looping and criss-crossing, "1776" in reed above the flag, and elaborate fancy work. A very unique piece, probably made for the nation's centennial. The cane work predates Heywood Brother's invention of set-in cane. Circa 1876.

A.: Natural lady's rocker with cane seat, star-caned back panel, and elaborate fancywork and circles on the back and scroll-work on the legs. Made by Heywood Brothers. Circa 1870s.

1880s

B.: Dark platform rocker with unique rolled arms, back, and legs, ball feet, and closely woven seat. White rocker with rolled arms and back, closely woven seat, and elaborate fancywork in the back. Platform rocker circa 1880s, rocker circa 1890s.

A.: White ornate platform rocker with closely woven seat, serpentine rolled arms and back, and scroll-laden lyre design on the back. White four-drawer baby's dressing stand with gesso on front of each drawer. Rocker circa 1880s, dressing stand circa 1910s.

B.: Natural rocker with cane seat, rolled serpentine arms and back, heart design on the back with unique weaving, and elaborate scrollwork and fancywork on the back and legs. Circa 1880s.

1890s

A.: Natural table with rolled wicker edge, wrapped legs and supports, and ball feet. Natural magazine rack with ball feet, wooden shelf, elegant scrollwork, and stick and ball work on the sides. Natural rocker with cane seat, star-caned panel on the back, scrollwork, and continuous ring design on the back. Table circa 1920s, magazine rack circa 1890s, and rocker circa 1890s.

B.: White open-weave rocker with cane seat and rolled arms and back. Victorian armchair with elaborate fancywork on the back and legs, cane seat, and beadwork along the top of the back. White fan motif rocker with star-caned fan, continuous ring design in the back, cane seat, and extensive loops and curlicues. Left rocker circa 1900s, center chair circa 1890s, right rocker circa 1880s.

A.: Natural rocker with serpentine rolled arms and back, closely woven seat, star caning in the back panel, stick and ball work, and scrollwork on the back and beneath the arms. Natural plant stand has rolled edge, wooden shelf, ball feet, and elaborate scrollwork. Natural platform rocker has rolled arms, closely woven seat, scrollwork on the back, and a combination of open-weave and close-weave work on the back. Rocker circa 1890s, plant stand circa 1900s, and platform rocker circa 1890s.

B.: Natural Victorian rocker with cane seat, stick and ball work, curlicues, diamond patterns on the back and extended skirt, and rolled arms and back. A beautiful piece. Circa 1880s.

C.: Natural rocker with round closely woven back panel, serpentine rolled arms and back, cane seat, and long skirt. Circa 1890s.

A.: Natural rocker with cane seat, rolled serpentine back and arms, patterned closely woven back panel, unusually high back, and fancy scrollwork. Circa 1890s.

B.: White ornate platform rocker with rolled serpentine arms and back, close-weave seat, ball feet, and close- and open-weave back. White sewing stand with hinged lid, wooden shelf, and close-weave design Rocker circa 1890s, sewing stand circa 1900s.

C.: White rocker with open-weave design, rolled arms and back, reed rings under the arms, and closely woven seat. White Victorian rocker with cane seat and very elaborate fancywork on the back. White rocker with cane seat, rolled arms and back, and open-weave design. Left rocker circa 1900s, center rocker circa 1890s, and right rocker circa 1900s.

A.: Natural Victorian round table with wooden top, ball and claw feet, and scrollwork and elaborate braiding in the legs. Lloyd's loom table lamp. Natural Victorian rocker with braided arms, cane seat, scrollwork and stick and ball work, and unique back panel design. Table circa 1880s, lamp circa 1920s, and rocker circa 1880s.

B.: Five-foot-tall floor lamp with close-weave base and shade and long fringe around the shade. Natural rocker with cane seat, rolled serpentine arms and back, scrollwork beneath the arms, and diamond pattern on the close-weave back section. Lamp circa 1900s, rocker circa 1890s.

C.: White round table with wooden top and shelf featuring braided wicker edging. White rocker with serpentine rolled arms and back and fancywork. Table circa 1900-1920, rocker circa 1890s.

A.: Natural Turkish bench with tight-weave seat, Aladdin's feet, unique spindles, swirling effect, and elegant fancywork. All original. Circa 1895.

B.: Natural wheelchair very similar to the one used in *FDR*. This one has larger front wheels and no hand rail on the back wheels. Circa 1890s.

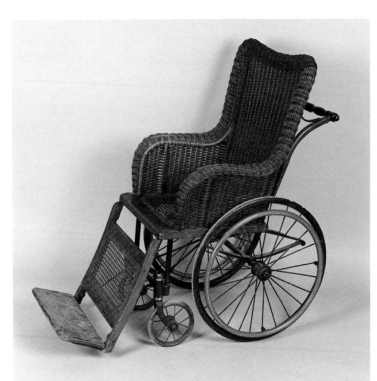

C.: Natural wheelchair with close-weave design, rolled arms and back, and cane seat and front panel for legs. This wheelchair was used in the movie *FDR*. Circa 1890s.

A.: White photographer's bench with heart design on the back, tight-weave seat, rolls, curlicues, and beadwork beneath the seat. Circa 1890s.

C.: Unique natural photographer's chair that actually is a Turkish bench with a removable back. Closely woven seat and back detail and lots of elaborate fancywork. Circa 1890s.

B.: Natural oversized Turkish bench with rolled arms, close-weave seat, stick and ball and scrollwork on the arms and around the legs. Circa 1890s.

1900s

A.: Natural armchair with rolled serpentine arms and back, open-weave and tight-weave design combined, and cane seat. Natural child's rocker with serpentine rolled arms and back, tightly woven back, stick and ball work in the back, and cane seat. Natural rocker with cane seat, rolled arms, continuous ring design around the back, and extensive hand-caning on the back. Left armchair circa 1900s, child's rocker circa 1900s, and right rocker circa 1890s.

B.: White rocker with combination open-weave and tight-weave design, closely woven seat, and cushion. White rocker with rolled serpentine arms and back, closely woven seat, and combination open-weave and close-weave back. Left rocker circa 1920s, right rocker circa 1900s.

C.: White rocker with cane seat, scrollwork, and prominent stick and ball work. White rocker with closely woven seat and braided open-weave work. Left rocker circa 1900s, right rocker circa 1920s.

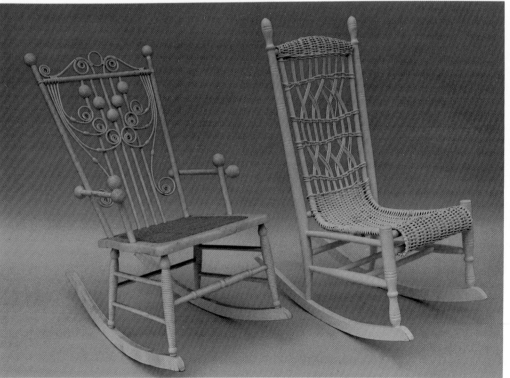

A.: White wheelchair with combination tight-weave and open-weave design, cane seat and front panel for legs, and rolled back and arms. Circa 1910s.

C.: White rocker with inner-spring floral cushion, open-weave sides, and unique inverted arrow designs on the back. Circa 1910s.

B.: Natural rocker with patterned cushion and backrest, very ornate scrollwork, and rolled back. Natural plant stand with wrapped legs, tight-weave design, and an unusual pattern on the side. Natural rattan table with wooden top. Rocker circa 1890-1910, plant stand circa 1920s, and table circa 1920s.

1920s

A.:Bar Harbor rocker with inner-spring cushion and close-weave arms, skirt, and upper back. White open-weave stand with four oak shelves and ball feet. Natural close-weave rocker with cane seat, serpentine arms and back, and scrollwork. Bar Harbor rocker circa 1910s, stand circa 1920s, and right rocker circa 1890s.

B.: Table with wicker skirt and wooden top and shelf. Rocker with wickerwork in the back and stick and ball work. Orange sewing basket with hinged lid, close-weave design, diamond pattern on the front, wooden shelf, and scrollwork on the wrapped legs. All pieces circa 1920s.

Sofas, Loveseats, Settees

A.: Victorian settee with painted cane seat and closely woven back. Two-tiered Victorian white end table. Natural Victorian table lamp has original silk fringe and lining. Settee circa 1880s, end table circa 1890s, lamp circa 1910s.

B.: White two-tiered smoking stand with cane-wrapped supports, white ornate loveseat with brown cushions and cane-wrapped supports, white ornate round table with bottom shelf, and green single-fixture lamp with woven reed frame. Loveseat has elaborate beadwork that forms an inverted triangle, and there is much scrollwork on the back and the cane-wrapped legs. Round table has painted wooden top and curlicues on legs. Smoking stand circa 1920s, loveseat circa 1880s, table circa 1880s, and lamp circa 1910s.

A.: White Victorian settee with natural cane seat, rolled arms, ornate scrollwork, excellent beadwork, and diamond patterns in serpentine back. White Victorian two-tiered table has scrollwork with balls and stained oak shelves. White table lamp has silk flowers in the shade and double bulb fixture. Settee and table circa 1880s, lamp circa 1910s.

B.: Very ornate white Victorian chair and loveseat, with serpentine back and arms. Diamond pattern in closely woven back of loveseat. Natural cane seat and elaborate fancywork on chair. Wrapped wooden legs on both pieces. Circa 1880s.

A.: Natural tea cart and white settee. Tea cart has a bottom shelf, tight-weave design, large wooden wheels, and a small basket for utensils by the handle. Settee has fancywork on the arms, serpentine arms and back, inverted triangles on the back, painted cane seat, a large skirt, and a combination of tight-weave and open-weave design. Tea cart circa 1900-1920, settee circa 1900s.

B: "Vanderbilt" natural loveseat with stick and ball and curlicue ornamentation and rolled back. Circa 1900s.

C.: White settee with serpentine back, legs, and arms, open-weave design in the back, and floral seat and backrest cushions. Circa 1900s.

1910s

A.: White loveseat with patterned cushion and white round table with woven bottom shelf. Loveseat has ball feet, arms, and back and very close weave. Table has wrapped legs and circular woven top. Both circa 1910-1930.

B.: White Bar Harbor sofa with floral inner-spring cushions and backrest. Part of a set including a chair. Circa 1915-1920.

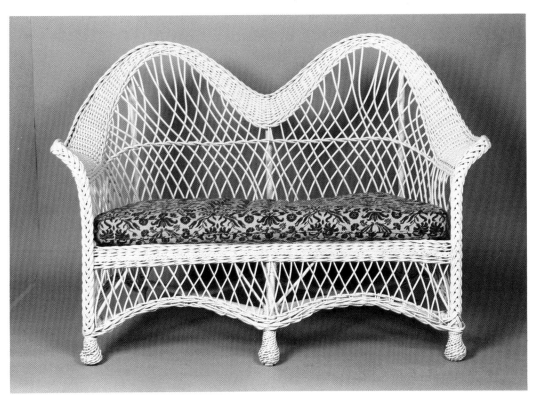

A.: White Bar Harbor loveseat with floral cushion and ball feet. Circa 1910s.

B.: White closely woven sofa with open-weave patterns in the back and skirt and matching floral cushions and pillows. Circa 1910s.

1920s

A.: Natural rattan sofa and chair with floral cushions. Circa 1920s.

B.: White Bar Harbor sofa with floral inner-spring cushions and inverted triangle designs in back and white table with wrapped legs and supports. Circa 1920s.

A.: White closely woven sofa with brown cushions and white tea cart with lift-off woven tray and white metal bottom shelf. Sofa circa 1920s, tea cart circa 1920s.

B.: Matching white open-weave armchair and settee with inner-spring brown cushions and close-weave rolled serpentine arms and back and ball feet. Circa 1910s.

C.: Art Deco natural sofa and child's chair. Sofa is part of a six-piece set including two chairs, a planter, a lamp, and a table. Sofa has diamond pattern in back and skirt. Circa 1920s.

A.: Closely woven sofa with unusual green, orange, and natural designs on the back; overstuffed cushions; and inner-spring seats. Circa 1920s.

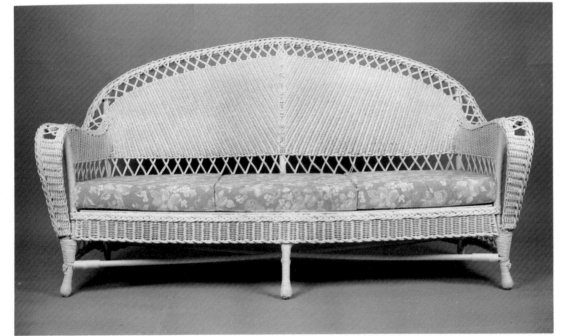

B.: White sofa with sectional floral cushions. Closely woven design with open-weave arm-rests. Circa 1920s.

C.: Green sofa with floral cushions. Closely woven design with diamond patterns woven into back and skirt. Circa 1920s.

A.: Natural sofa with floral cushions and inner springs. Closely woven design with diamond patterns in the back, rolled arms, and cane-wrapped legs. Circa 1910s.

B.: White sofa with plaid mattress, diamond patterns on the back, and long skirt. Closely woven design. Circa 1920s.

C.: White open-weave loveseat with green floral cushions and backrest and ball feet. Circa 1920s.

A.: White sofa with diamond patterns on the back and skirt and matching floral cushions and pillows. Inner springs in the seat. Closely woven design. Seven feet in length. Circa 1920s.

B.: Matching natural sofa and armchair with floral cushions. Both have tightly woven design, large skirts, inner springs in the seats, and diamond patterns on their mildly arched backs. Circa 1920s.

C.: White closely woven sofa with blue patterned cushions and orange pillow, ball feet, and inner springs in seat. Circa 1920s.

A.: Matching beige sofa and rocker with rust-colored cushions (with inner springs on the sofa seat). Inverted triangle designs within white and red bands on backs of both pieces. Tightly woven design. Circa 1920s.

B.: Matching brown sofa and rocker with patterned cushions. Inverted triangle design on backs of both pieces. Combination open-weave and tight-weave style. Circa 1920s.

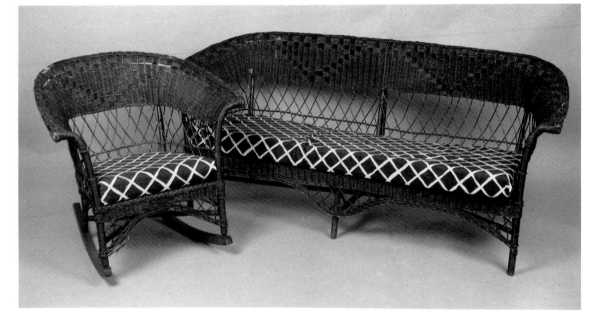

C.: White Victorian armchair, white shelves, and white settee. Armchair has a cane seat (beneath the green cushion), serpentine back and arms, and elaborate fancywork on the arms and skirt. The shelves are painted oak with wicker legs and supports. The settee has serpentine arms and back, inverted triangles on the back, painted cane seat, and both open-weave and tight-weave work on the back and arms. Armchair circa 1890s, stand circa 1910s, and settee circa 1920s.

Loungers

1880s

A.: Natural lounge with rush woven seat, orange cushion, and elaborate fancywork along the sides and ends. Made by Heywood Brothers and Wakefield Rattan Company. Circa 1880s.

1890s

B.:Natural deck chair with floral cushions, adjustable back, ball feet, and elaborate fancywork. A beautiful piece. Circa 1890s.

A.: White floor lamp with tightly woven six-sided base and fancy column, and floral fabric shade. White lounge has reed circles on the back, cane seat, rolled arm, and elaborate fancywork on the back and legs. Floor lamp circa 1910s, lounge circa 1890s.

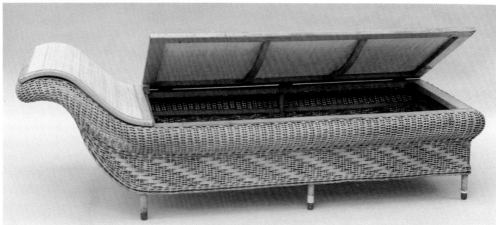

B. and C.: Natural fainting couch with blanket chest featuring a hinged lid, cane seat and headrest, rolled edges, and a close, patterned weave on the sides. A very rare piece. Made by Heywood Brothers and Wakefield Rattan Company. Circa 1890s.

1910s

A.: Natural end table with wooden top and shelf, wrapped legs, and ballwork beneath lower shelf. Orange tight-weave lounge has black, green and orange diamond pattern on the back, footrest, and uneven arms. Table circa 1900s, lounge circa 1910s.

B.: Small white table with circular woven top, open-weave sides, and ball feet. White Bar Harbor chaise lounge with ball feet. White plant stand with reed circles, wood and wicker top, and scrollwork around the base. Table circa 1910s, chaise lounge circa 1910s, and plant stand circa 1900s.

C.: Natural Bar Harbor chaise lounge with braided arms and back, ball feet, and magazine holder on left arm. Circa 1910s.

A.: White lounge chair with tight-weave design, set-in cane seat, serpentine and braided arms and back, and braidwork on the footrest and around the top and bottom of the skirt. Circa 1910s.

B.: Natural bed with double twisting on the posts make it earlier than its simple lines make it appear. Made by Heywood Brothers and Wakefield Rattan Company. Circa 1910s.

1920s

A.: Dark green rattan lounge chair. White floor lamp with tight-weave base and column and combination tight-weave and open-weave shade. Both pieces circa 1920s.

B.: White Bar Harbor lounge chair with close-weave seat, flat woven arms, footrest, and ball feet. Circa 1920s.

C.: White daybed with blue mattress and cushions, ball feet, and combination open-weave and tight-weave design. Circa 1920s.

A.: White oval table with wooden top, tight-weave side and legs, woven shelf, and diamond patterns on the legs. White Bar Harbor lounge chair with floral mattress, tight-weave seat and back section, and diamond pattern on the back. Table circa 1910s, lounge chair circa 1920s.

B.: Natural lounge chair with blue cushions, tight-weave design, and adjustable ottoman with footrest. Flat woven arms have spaces for drinks and magazines. Circa 1930s.

Sets

Opposite page:
Dining room. Six-sided pedestal table with oak top and wicker skirt. Chairs from a collection of reception chairs with various motifs. Corner hanging whatnot shelf with stick and ball and curlicue was restored. Table circa 1910s, chairs circa 1890s.

Living room group. Green stain originals with some restorations. Horseshoe-back set, heart basket, tea cart, ottoman, planter, end table all from the 1890s except for the tall stand (1910s). Mostly Heywood Brothers and Wakefield Rattan Company.

A.: Matching white armchair and rocker with cushions, flat woven arms, overall close-weave design, and ball feet on the armchair. Circa 1910s.

B.: White sofa with combination open-weave and tight-weave back and arms. Inner springs in seat, patterned cushions, and ball feet. Part of a set including two chairs. Circa 1910s.

A.: Matching white open-weave armchair and rocker have green cushions and close-weave back panel with diamond patterns. White rectangular table has wooden top and wrapped legs. All pieces circa 1910s.

B.: White sofa with sectional green cushions and arrow tip patterns in back. Part of a set including chairs. Circa 1910s.

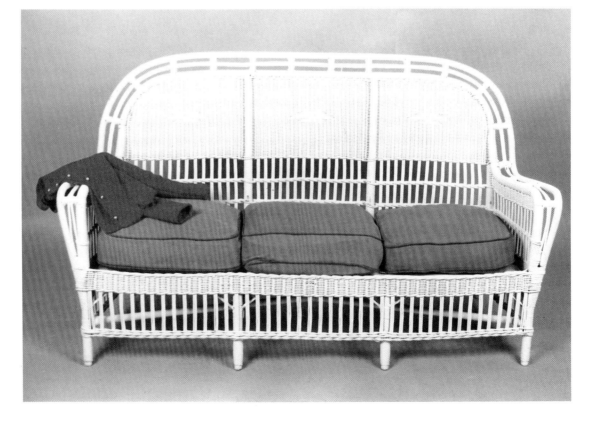

A.: Natural closely woven sofa
with open weave rectangles in
the back and a green strip along
the skirt. Overstuffed patterned
cushions and orange pillows.
Unusual design. Circa 1920s.

B.: Matching natural rocker and
armchair with striped floral
cushions, flat woven arms,
close-weave design, and
rectangular open-weave
pattern on the backs. Natural
oval table has green wooden
top, close-weave design, and
square base. All pieces circa
1910s.

A.: White matching armchair and rocker with a white floor lamp. Armchair and rocker have floral cushions with inner springs beneath, long skirts, flat woven arms, and close-weave design except for the open-weave work on the backs. Lamp has woven shade and base and wrapped column. All pieces circa 1910s.

B.: White sofa combining closely woven skirt and lower back with open-weave back. With floral mattress and pink and green pillows. Features a long skirt and inner springs in the seat. Circa 1915-1925.

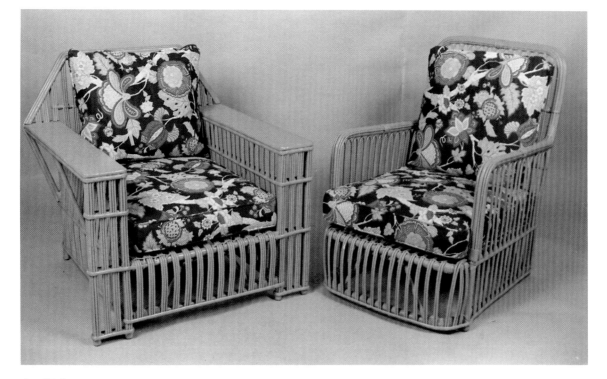

A.: Light green rattan armchairs, one with solid wood
armrests. Both have floral
cushions and backrests. Circa
1920s.

B.: Matching light green rattan
sofa with floral cushions and
painted hardwood armrests
and table with painted hardwood top. Circa 1920s.

1920s

A.: White closely woven armchair with diamond patterns on the back and long skirt, with a floral cushion and inner springs under the seat. Part of a set including a sofa. Circa 1920s.

B.: White sofa with innerspring floral cushions, wrapped legs, and diamond patterns on the back and skirt. Closely woven design. Circa 1920s.

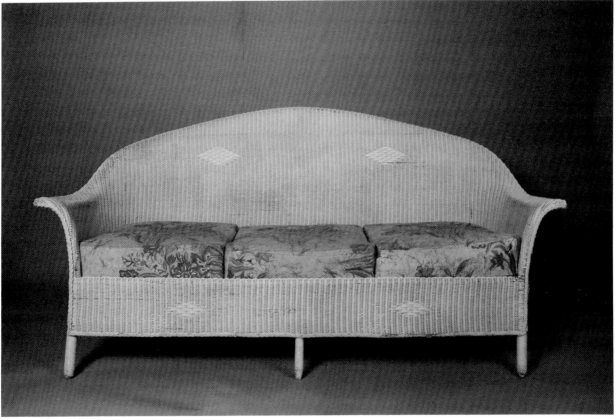

A.: Matching green sofa and lamp. Sofa has closely woven design, arches in individual back sections, and diamond patterns and open-weave work on the back. Lamp has silk-lined shade and open-weave work on the base. Both circa 1920s.

B.: Matching green armchair and rocker with close-weave design, flat woven arms, floral cushions, diamond and open-weave patterns in the back, and a long skirt in back on the armchair. Oval green table has a wooden top and woven shelf. All pieces circa 1920s.

DRYAD CANE FURNITURE

EVE'S CUSHION GROUP

NO. 394	NO. 576	NO. 575	NO. 57
SETTEE	TABLE	ROCKER	CHAIR
Total height 32 in., total width 57½ in., height of seat from ground 16 in., depth of seat 20 in., length of seat between arms 42 in.	Height 28 in., diameter 26 in. Cane top.	Total height 31½ in., total width 32 in., height of seat from ground 17½ in., depth of seat 17½ in.	Total height 31½ in., total width 32 in., height of seat from ground 17½ in., depth of seat 19 in.
£9 . 17 . 6	£3 . 17 . 6 With glass top and brass clips £4 . 18 . 6 Teak or oak top £3 . 7 . 6	£5 . 0 . 0	£4 . 17 . 6

Most chairs can be fitted with rockers if desired

558

Hand Woven Genuine Reed Furniture At Factory Prices

EXPERTLY MADE AND EXCELLENTLY FINISHED.   **ATTRACTIVELY PRICED IN THIS SELLING**
    The **PLAIN FINISHES** are: Light or Dark Baronial Brown. The **FANCY FINISHES** are: Old Ivory, Frosted Brown. Blue and Gold, Green and Gold, French Gray, Silvertone Black and Blootan (Tan with a blue rub).
BE SURE TO SPECIFY FINISH WANTED WHEN ORDERING

Made of genuine reed, hand woven. Entire suite is remarkably low priced in this selling. Suitable for any room in the home. Resilient and comfortable. Covered with a fine grade Cretonne in an attractive design.

"A" No. 3VA21 Reed Chair. Spring filled cushion on coiled spring seat. Seat, 19x19 inches. Back, 22 inches high.
Plain Finish, each..........$21.45   Fancy Finish, each............$24.00

"B" No. 3VA21 Reed Settee. 40 inches wide. Spring filled cushion on coiled spring seat. Seat, 21x40 inches. Back, 22 inches high. (Also made in widths, 48 and 60 inches. Lowest factory prices assured in event the larger sizes are wanted.)
Plain Finish, each............ 38.50   Fancy Finish, each............$41.90

"C" No. 3VA21 Reed Table round. Five-ply wood top. Diameter, 24 inches. Table top enameled or stained to match finish on reed work.
Plain Finish, each............$15.10   Fancy Finish, each............$16.40

"D" No. 3VA21 Reed Table Lamp. Has silk lined shade. Height, 20 inches. Diameter of shade, 18 inches. 2-light pull chain cluster, silk cord and plug.
Plain Finish, each............$32.45   Fancy Finish, each............$34.50

"E" No. 3VA21 Reed Day Bed. Spring filled cushions on coiled spring seat. Seat, 30x72 inches.
Plain Finish, each...............$67.05   Fancy Finish, each............$72.15

"F" No. 3VA21 Reed Rocker. Spring filled cushion on coiled spring seat. Seat, 19x19 inches. Back, 18 inches high.
Plain Finish, each............$21.45   Fancy Finish, each............$24.00

"G" No. 3VA21 Reed Bird Cage and Standard. Cage has removable metal pan and seed cups. Height, 72 inches.
Plain Finish, each............$17.00   Fancy Finish, each............$17.55

DESCRIPTION AND PRICES OF PIECES NOT SHOWN

No. 3VA21 Reed Davenport, 72 inches wide. Spring filled cushion on coiled spring seat. Seat, 21x72 inches. Back, 22 inches high.
Plain Finish, each.............$63.85   Fancy Finish, each............$68.95

No. 3VA21 Reed Chaise Longue. Spring filled cushion on coiled spring seat. Seat, 21x50 inches. Back, 18 inches high.
Plain Finish, each............$45.45   Fancy Finish, each............$50.55

1880s

A.: Green floor lamp with open-weave shade and pink silk lining. Natural Victorian oval table with oak top and bottom shelf, serpentine design, beadwork, and a lot of character. Green table lamp has open-weave shade and pink silk lining. Floor lamp and table lamp circa 1900s, table circa 1880s.

1890s

B.: Natural Victorian center square table with wooden top and shelf, rolled edge, and double twisted wrap. Made by Wakefield Rattan Company. Circa 1890s.

Chapter 5

Tables and Desks

A.: Natural tea table with stick and ball and curlicue details, oak top and serving shelves, and wrapped legs with balls. Circa 1890s.

B.: Natural center square Victorian table with set-in cane top, rolled skirt, double twisting, and bird cage work in the center of the pedestal. Attributed to Heywood Brothers. Circa 1890s.

C.: Green, orange, and natural tea table with green turtle top plus stick and ball and curlicue details. Made by Heywood Brothers. Circa 1890s.

1900s

A.: Light blue three-tiered stand with rolled edge and curlicues and cane shelves. Circa 1900s.

1910s

C.: White end table with cane top and shelf. Large white reed planter-type piece was used as a prop in Woody Allen's *Stardust Memories*. Both pieces circa 1920s.

B.: White desk with wooden drawer, gallery, wooden top, and closely woven design. Natural table lamp has open-weave shade and silk fringe. Both pieces circa 1910s.

A.: White Bar Harbor armchair with wrapped legs, floral cushion and backrest, and flat woven armrests. White round table with circular woven top and shelf, wrapped legs, and ball feet. Armchair circa 1920s, table circa 1910s.

B.: Center square table combining oak top, wicker, and hickory. Strong Adirondack influence. Circa 1910s.

C.: Rattan end table with original paint and wrapped legs. Circa 1910s.

A.: Two white end tables with stained oak tops and wrapped legs. Table on right has open-weave skirt and woven shelf. Both pieces circa 1920s.

B.: White armchair with open-weave design, cane seat, and intricate curlicues on the back, arms, skirt, and leg supports. White oval table with open-weave skirt, wooden top and wrapped legs. Armchair circa 1890s, table circa 1910s.

C.: Natural telephone stand with wooden top and shelf from Heywood-Wakefield. Two-piece set has unique place for stick phone and a stool with woven seat. Circa 1910s.

1920s

A.: White rectangular table with stained oak top and wooden shelf. White planter with open-weave arch, tight-weave plant holders and shelf, and diamond patterns on the side. Table circa 1910s, planter circa 1920s.

B.: Art Deco library table with original paint featuring painted and woven chevron on the top, diamond patterns on the sides and woven shelf, and wrapped legs. Circa 1920s.

C.: Dark brown close-weave desk with oak top, woven shelf, and wrapped legs. White table lamp has open-weave shade. Both pieces circa 1920s.

A.: Natural sewing table with wooden drawer, two hinged lids (one on each side), two baskets, a bottom shelf, and a combination of tight-weave and open-weave work on the baskets. Circa 1920s.

C.: White rectangular table with woven top and shelf, braided edge, and ball feet. Circa 1920s.

B.: White rectangular table with close-weave design and woven shelf. Circa 1920s.

Chapter 6
Children's Furniture

A.: Natural baby carriage has rolled edges with stick and ball and curlicues, starburst design, and wooden wheels. Green velvet on the inside of the carriage. Circa 1890s.

B.: Natural baby carriage in a shell design—almost like a slipper—with intricate scrollwork and wire wheels. Circa 1890s.

C.: Natural three-piece baby swing cradle including crown, cradle, and stand. Cradle sides look like butterfly wing. Attributed to Heywood Brothers. Circa 1895.

D.: White Victorian junior chair with fiddleback design with star caning plus a star and bow. Attributed to Wakefield Rattan Company. Circa 1890s.

A.: White junior chair with star-caned fan back and continuous ring design and cane seat. Attributed to Wakefield Rattan Company. Circa 1890s.

B.: Natural doll's swing cradle, all original, with crown piece and finials. Circa 1890s.

A.: White child's rocker that is a variation of the horseshoe style. Rolled arms, stick and ball and curlicue features. Attributed to Heywood Brothers and Wakefield Rattan Company. Circa 1898.

B.: White ornate child's chair with double twisting and curlicues and cane seat. A rare piece. Circa 1890s.

C.: Natural child's heart rocker with hand caning, stick and ball work and curlicues. Attributed to Heywood Brothers and Wakefield Rattan Company. Circa 1898.

1900s

A.: White laundry hamper with hinged lid, close-weave design, diamond pattern weave on the front, and handles. White commode with wooden seat and lid, cane panel in the back and caning around the sides. White child's rocker with fan motif in back featuring star caning and elaborate scrollwork. Hamper circa 1900-1920, commode circa 1890-1910, and rocker circa 1880s.

B.: White child's washstand with divided washbowl featuring cherubs and handles for washcloths. Woven shelf at bottom. Circa 1900s.

C.: White baby dressing stand in tightly woven design. Very unique—it has gesso on all four sides. Circa 1910s.

1910s

A.: White hooded bassinet with closely woven design, wooden wheels, and gesso on the sides. Circa 1910s.

B.: Restored white high chair with removable tray and gesso. Circa 1915.

C.: White crib with combination of tight- and open-weave design and wrapped legs. Circa 1910s.

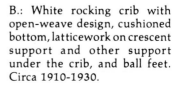

A.: Two small white dining chairs. Chair on left has cane seat, close-weave design, diamond pattern on the back, and is part of a four-piece set. Chair in middle has close-weave design. White baby's layette with close-weave design. Chairs circa 1900s, layette circa 1910s.

B.: White rocking crib with open-weave design, cushioned bottom, latticework on crescent support and other support under the crib, and ball feet. Circa 1910-1930.

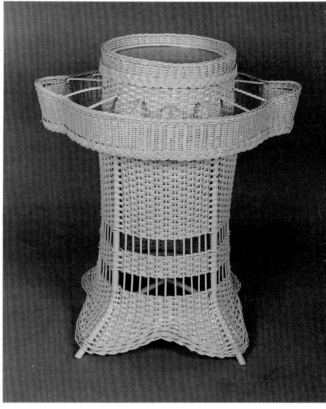

A.: Small crib with gesso on all four sides and one adjustable side. All original (discounting the animals). Circa 1910s.

B.: White bassinet with pink and blue gesso (original paint), close-weave design, silk hood and ribbons, and wooden wheels. Circa 1910s.

C.: White serving stand/tea tray with lift-off top and tin insert for wine and ice. Tightly woven design. Circa 1910s.

1920s

A.: Natural tight-weave child's armchair with painted design on the back. Unique open-weave baby scale (up to twenty-five pounds). Natural woven reed basket with tin insert. All pieces circa 1920s.

B.: White baby carriage with close-weave design and diamond pattern on the sides. Wire wheels with rubber tires. Circa 1920s.

C.: White crib with fancywork on headboard and footboard, wrapped legs, and open-weave design. Circa 1920s.

Chapter 7

Throughout the House

1880s

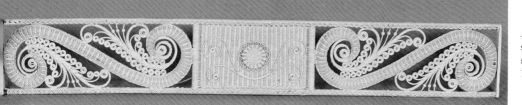

A.: White fretwork with rolled scrollwork, applied work, and stick and ball details. Circa 1890s.

B.: White Turkish bench with tight-weave patterned seat, rolled arms, bird cage details on the legs, and scrollwork and beadwork on the arms and legs. Circa 1880s.

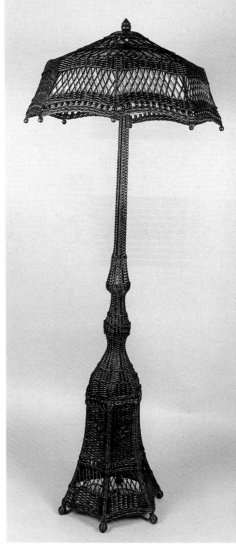

D.: Natural Victorian floor lamp with stick and ball work, curlicues, and open-weave shade with silk lining. Circa 1880s.

C.: Natural windmill fire screen with four types of hand caning on the blades. Circa 1890s.

1890s

A.: White fire screen with ornate stick and ball and curlicue work and uniquely wrapped side posts. White flower baskets are tightly woven with gesso applied. All circa 1890s.

B.: Natural and black fire screen with unique braided caning. Circa 1880s.

C.: Natural whatnot with arched top, multilevel oak shelves, elaborate fancywork, unique wrapping on the columns, and beadwork. Circa 1890s.

A.: Natural easel with harp inset, stick and ball work, and scrollwork. Circa 1890s.

C.: Natural whatnot with three oak shelves, stick and ball work, and curlicues. Circa 1898.

B.: Natural whatnot with four oak shelves, stick and ball work, and curlicues. Circa 1890s.

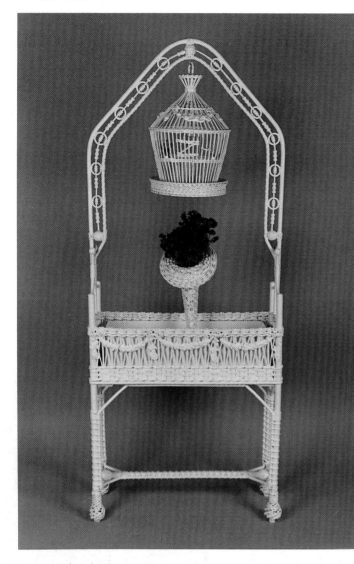

B.: Crested shelf with double twisted finials and curlicues and loops. Circa 1890s.

A.: White bird cage planter with gesso, ornate fancywork, and curlicues. An early piece. Circa 1890s.

1900s

C.: Green desk with gallery. Features original green paint, lots of compartments, drawers, and shelves, and pull-out shelf for typewriter. Early weaving on drawers, sides, and tops. Circa 1900s.

A.: Natural hat rack with close-weave design, diamond patterns on the base, and wrapped columns. Orange log carrier with wooden bottom, close weaving, and stick and ball work. Black chair with cane seat, serpentine back, star caning on the back, and open-weave skirt. Hat rack circa 1910s, log carrier circa 1890-1910, and chair circa 1880-1900.

B. and C.: White Victrola with tight-weave design, hinged lid, and doors opening onto storage space for music. Circa 1900s.

B.: Natural double floor lamp with painted green trim, close-weave base, and open-weave shades. Circa 1910s.

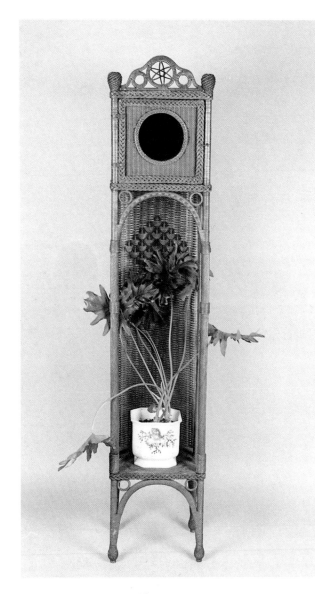

A.: Natural, green, and bronze grandfather clock case with tight-weave design, ball feet, scrollwork, and diamond pattern in the back. Circa 1900s.

C.: Six-drawer lingerie chest with tight-weave design and cane and gesso. Circa 1920s.

A.: White corner clock etagere with clock case featuring brass numerals and space for a pendulum, double-twisted finials, wooden shelves, and curlicues. Circa 1910s.

B. and C.: Natural Edison Victrola with cabinet for extra music. Tight-weave design with ball feet, diamond patterns on the sides, and a unique pattern on the cabinet door. Circa 1915.

1920s

A.: White desk/table with two woven shelves on each end and open-weave work on the sides. White coat rack with wrapped columns. Both pieces circa 1920s.

B.: Close-weave dresser with five drawers and one door. A rare piece. Circa 1900s.

A.: Light blue Art Deco tea cart with tight-weave design, leaf pattern in the cutout, woven shelf, wrapped legs, and lift-out tray. Circa 1920s.

B.: White Lloyd's loom planter with bird cage holder (not seen here), wooden shelf, and scroll-work in the arch. Circa 1920s.

C.: White circular plant stand with tight-weave design and wooden bottom shelf with a skirt. Brown tea cart featuring wooden drop leaf top, wooden wheels with rubber tread, and wooden shelf with braided wicker trim. Plant stand circa 1910s, tea cart circa 1920s.

D.: Natural tea cart with two shelves with braided edges and wrapped legs and supports. Circa 1920s.

Exchange, Craig Hall, South Illinois Avenue, Atlantic City, N. J.

HOTEL ENDICOTT SUN PARLOR

Chapter 8
Wicker Care and Restoration

Cleaning

Basic maintenance of *natural, unpainted* antique wicker furniture is simple. Periodic dusting with the dust brush attachment on your vacuum cleaner will keep the pieces clean. Beyond that, an annual spraying with a garden hose (preferably in the backyard) will help remove more stubborn dust and dirt and keep the natural fibers of wicker furniture supple and resilient. The idea of taking one's prized antique wicker pieces out to the yard for a shower may seem odd and even foolhardy (you wouldn't do it to your Chippendale dining chair set). Remember, however, that the raw materials that make up the furniture— willow, reed, cane, rattan—grew in wetlands, so they're used to water. If you can't get the furniture outside or don't have an outside to take the furniture to, a thorough cleaning with an old toothbrush and warm soapy water will suffice. In fact, for really stubborn dirt, you may want to use the soapy water and a toothbrush outside (if possible) before spraying the piece. Even if your wicker pieces seem perfectly clean and you don't feel that an annual shower is in order, it may be beneficial nonetheless. Sit on your chairs and sofas and prod your other pieces. If they creak and groan, they may be drying out. Nothing will restore them better than a shower or a thorough "sponge bath" with a soft wet cloth or sponge. Discolored or very badly soiled pieces can be cleaned with a toothbrush dipped in a weak domestic bleach solution. Be very careful when doing this. Try this method on the underside of a piece to check the results before cleaning exposed areas. Too much bleach can leave you with a two-tone Victorian wicker chair that may not be to your liking.

Painted wicker furniture (the majority of antique pieces were painted) may be cleaned in the ways already mentioned. However, you carefully must determine the materials used in your painted pieces before beginning to clean them. If the pieces were made of Oriental sea grass and other grasses, don't give them a shower, just use a damp cloth or sponge. If the furniture was made of man-made fiber, *do not* get them wet, even if they were heavily painted. A shower could leave your fiber chair looking like a soggy mass of kraft paper that only vaguely resembles a wicker chair. A damp cloth or sponge will be sufficient to clean fiber pieces.

Restoring

Simple repairs can be done by anyone handy with tools. Among those necessary are a hammer, screwdrivers, needle-nose pliers, a mat knife, clamps, clippers, a chisel, and scissors. Supplies include white glue, rags for wiping excess glue, raw replacement materials, and nails (preferable one-half to three-quarter-inch in length with heads). The raw materials used to replace broken or missing pieces on your furniture can be obtained from a craft supply house. Take a sample of material from the section of the furniture you wish to repair to the supply house and have them match it as closely as possible.

Before beginning, soak the raw material in water to make it flexible. Cane used in repairs should be soaked for five minutes and reed (depending on thickness) from ten to twenty minutes. Insufficiently soaked material will break; overly soaked reed will fray. The three most simple wicker repair jobs are (1) rewrapping legs, (2) replacing broken spokes, and (3) replacing horizontal reeds.

1. To rewrap the leg of a wicker chair, begin by soaking the binder cane for five minutes (or until flexible). Turn the chair upside down for easy access to the legs. Unwrap damaged or loosened old cane to a point where it is in good condition. At that point, nail down the end of the old cane to insure that it stays in place. Try to position the nail so that it is not visible from the front of the chair. Apply glue the length of the area to be covered, and spread it fairly thinly (so that it does not run).

Take a length of the pre-soaked new cane and nail the end of it adjacent to where the old cane ends. Wrap it evenly and tightly from that point to the bottom of the leg and nail it roughly one-quarter of an inch from the end of the leg. If the chair has brass (or other metal) caps on the ends of the legs, wind the replacement cane to the cap. If you think the cap can be removed and the cane secured beneath the cap, try it. However, don't force the cap off if it is secure and don't try to force it back on if the cane will not fit beneath it.

2. Spokes, the vertical supports on the back of a wicker chair that are interwoven with horizontal reeds, are wicker's equivalent to the human skeleton. Unfortunately, they cannot be set like bones when they break. To replace a spoke, cut the broken spoke at the top, where it ends beneath the horizontal reed rows. Then at its lower end cut it three or four rows below where it interweaves with the horizontal reed. Measure the replacement spoke to approximately the same length as the spoke you removed. Cut it to size. Insert the new, pre-soaked vertical reed spoke in place of the broken one, threading it bottom first and then at the top. You may have trouble fitting the new spoke into the horizontal weave. If so, cut the ends of the new spoke into points, but don't shorten them and don't make them so sharp that they cut the existing weave. Bend the spoke as necessary as you place it so that you can insert it into the horizontal weave at the top and bottom. Make sure that the new spoke fits snugly and is close to the same length as the one you removed. While keeping the new spoke in place, take the ends out. Put glue on both ends. Return them to their place in the top and bottom of the horizontal weave. Allow the glue to dry.

3. Replacing horizontal reed is a process similar to replacing spokes. Pre-soak the replacement reed. Cut out the damaged horizontal weave. Approximate the length of the new piece, and thread it through the vertical spokes using the over/under pattern utilized on the other horizontal reeds. Make sure that it fits in the weave snugly and is the proper length. Put glue on the ends of the horizontal reed. Tuck the glued ends into the pre-existing weave. Allow this work to dry and stiffen before moving on to any other repairs.

If your furniture needs major repair, or any repair much more complex than those described, seek a restoration specialist. Don't risk ruining a valuable, one-of-a-kind antique if you're not sure how to repair it. A restoration specialist will be able to assess the damage and tell you whether or not the piece is worth repairing.

Restoring wicker furniture should be done after removing any paint or other finish and preferably before repainting, coating, or staining it. That is why it is important to have new replacement materials match the existing wicker as closely as possible. A well-restored antique wicker piece will be indistinguishable from an unrestored but perfectly kept piece to all but the most discerning eye.

Refinishing

If you plan to restore the finish of a painted wicker piece, first consult a professional with experience in this field. Again, it is important to know what raw material(s) were used to make the furniture. Man-made fiber and Oriental sea grass pieces should not be refinished because the chemicals used in the process literally will eat away the materials. Furnishings made from cane, rattan, reed, and willow can be refinished successfully as long as care is used. Dried-out or brittle pieces should not be refinished at all, as they may be destroyed. (Seek a professional's advice on further care for such pieces.) Hand refinishing is not recommended for pieces with lots of detail, as chances are that some areas will receive too much and other areas too little of the finish-removing chemicals. More simple designs (open-weave pieces, for example) can be successfully refinished with care, patience, a toothbrush, and a pointed (but not too sharp) implement such as an awl.

One option for removing old finishes is dipping the entire piece into a large vat of chemicals, known as a "stripping" tank. If you choose this method over the laborious hand-rubbing method, do not leave the furniture in the vat until *all* of the paint is off, as reed will fray and permanent damage can be done. Leave it in just long enough so that most of the paint comes off, then use a toothbrush and awl to remove paint still adhering to tight corners and crevices. If your wicker piece has an original paper or metal label on the bottom, dip-stripping is not recommended because the label may be destroyed or irreparably damaged.

Wicker furnishings that have had an old finish removed may be coated, stained, or painted. A protective coating especially is important if the wicker furnishings will be used on a regular basis, because the porous materials can be soiled easily. Clear lacquer, linseed oil, mineral oil, orange shellac, or clear varnish are recommended. Most hardware stores carry these products except for the orange shellac, which may take some time to find. Orange shellac is highly recommended because it lets the wicker breathe and yet seals it at the same time. All coatings can be applied by brush or with a sprayer, which provides more even results if done properly. Stains can be used as well, but if you wish to match the finish of existing pieces, test the stain on the underside of the piece, let it dry, and compare the new finish with the other pieces.

Wicker can be painted regardless of the raw materials used (although rattan doesn't take paint quite as well as other materials). High-grade enamel, acrylic enamel, oil-based paints, or wicker craft paint (an enamel paint attainable through craft supply stores) are recommended. Do not use latex paint. If a piece to be painted is currently without finish, remember that it may be more valuable in its natural state. Consider its long-range use. You may want to use lacquer, shellac, or varnish instead or stain the piece instead of painting it. If it already is painted, remove chipping paint and clean the piece thoroughly. Wicker craft paint must be applied with a brush; enamels are available in aerosol form or may be used with a compressor.

Restoring, stripping and refinishing can be done at home if you have the space, the inclination, the know-how, and the time. If you have any question or doubts about the task at hand, call a professional. If you don't know of one in your area, check with antique wicker dealers. Most of them are familiar with refinishers and restorers who may do work for them.

Photo Credits

Photographs were taken by the author, unless otherwise noted, from the following collections:

A Summer Place, 37 Boston Street, Guilford, Connecticut: page 8; 11 A, B, and C; 14 A, B, and C; 15; 16 A, B, and C; 18 A, B, and C; 19 A, B, and C; 20 A and B; 21 A and B; 22; 24 A and B; 25 B; 26 A and B; 27 B; 35 A and B; 36 A and B; 45 B; 53 A and B; 54 A, B, and C; 55 A and B; 58 B and C; 59 B; 60 A and B; 61 A and B; 71 C; 85 A; 86 C; 92 A and C; 93 A, B, and C; 101 B; 110 B; 113 M; 116; 117; 126 B; 127 A, B, and C; 128 A; 129 B; 130 C; 131 B; 134 A, B, and C; 135 A and B; 136 A, B, C, and D; 137 A, B, an A and B; 141 A, B, and C; 143 A, C, and D; 144 A, B, and C; 145 A, B, and C; 146 A, B, and C; 148 A and B; 149 A and B; 151 A.

Saugerties Auction Services, 16 Livingston Street, Saugerties, New York: page 1; 25 A; 28 B; 32 A; 33 A and B; 37 A and B; 38 A and B; 39 A and B; 41 A and B; 66 B; 67 B; 68 A; 69 A and B; 70 A, B, and C; 71 A; 72 A, B, and C; 73 A, B, and C; 74 A, B, and C; 75 A, B, and C; 76 A and B; 77 C; 78 A; 79 A, B, and C; 80 A; 81 A, B, and C; 82 B; 83 A and C; 84 A and C; 85 B; 86 B; 87 A; 88 A and B; 89 A; 90 B and C; 91 C; 94 A and B; 95 A; 96 A, B, and C; 97 B and C; 98 A and B; 99 B; 101 A; 102 A and B; 103 A and B; 104 A and B; 105 A, B, and C; 106 A, B, and C; 107 A, B, and C; 108 A, B, and C; 109 A, B, and C; 111 A; 112 A and B; 113 A; 114 A, B, and C; 115 A; 118 A and B; 119 A and B; 120 A and B; 121 A and B; 122 A and B; 123 A and B; 124 A and B; 129 A; 130 B; 131 A and C; 132 A, B, and C; 133 A, B, and C; 138 A; 139 C; 142 B and C; 147 A; 150 A; 151 D.

Oley Valley Country Store, 2 East Philadelphia Avenue, Boyertown, Pennsylvania: page 30 B, 32 B, 34 A, 68 C, 71 B, 77 B, 78 B, 80 B, 82 B, 84 B, 91 B, 92 B, 94 C, 95 C, 97 A, 100 B, 101 C, 111 B and C, 112 C, 128 C, 129 C, 130 A, 140 A and B, 142 A, 147 B and C, 150 B.

Bill Sharon Collection: (Most of which were made available through Oley Valley Country Store.) Page 56, 58 A, 59 A, 66 A and C, 67 A, 69 C, 77 A, 83 B, 86 A, 87 B, 89 B and C, 90 A, 91 A, 99 A, 100 A, 110 A, 115 B, 126 A, 128 B, 143 B, 151 B and C.

H. Blairman and Sons, Ltd., London: page 27 A.

Maxine's: page 68 B.

Hursman: page 95 B.

Peabody Museum, East India Square, Salem, Massachusetts: page 4, 8, 9, 23.

Ficks Reed Company, Cincinnati, Ohio: page 47, 63, 65.

William B. Johns and Partners, Ltd., New York: page 49.

Richard Greenwood, *The Five Heywood Brothers*: page 51, 61.

H.H. Perkins Company, 125 Bradley Road, Woodbridge, Connecticut: page 6.

Bibliography

A Completed Century, The Story of the Heywood-Wakefield Company, 1826-1926. Boston: The Heywood-Wakefield Company, 1926.

Patricia Corbin, *All About Wicker*. New York: E.P Dutton, 1978.

Thomas Duncan, *How to Buy and Restore Wicker Furniture*. Syracuse, Indiana: Duncan-Holmes Publishing Co., 1983.

Richard N. Greenwood, *The Five Heywood Brothers, A Brief History of the Heywood-Wakefield Company During 125 Years*. New York: The Newcomen Society, 1951.

Kathryn Boyd Menz, *Wicker in the American Home*. Newark, Del.: University of Delaware, 1976.

Bruce W. Miller and Jim Widess, *The Caner's Handbook*. New York: Prentice Hall Press, 1983.

Richard Saunders, *Collecting and Restoring Wicker Furniture*. New York: Crown Publishers, Inc., 1976.

Richard Saunders, *Collector's Guide to American Wicker Furniture*. New York: Hearst Books, 1983.

Richard Saunders, *The Official Price Guide to Wicker*. New York: The House of Collectibles, 1988.

G.E. Shirley, *Great Grandmother's Wicker Furniture, 1880-1920s*. Burlington, Iowa: Craftsman Press, 1979.

Robert W. and Harriet Swedberg, *Wicker Furniture Styles and Prices*. Lombard, Illinois: Wallace-Homestead Book Co., 1983.

Jeffrey Weiss, *Cornerstone Collector's Guide to Wicker*. New York: Cornerstone Library (Simon and Schuster), 1981.

Price Guide for *Fine Wicker Furniture: 1870-1930*

Values vary immensely according to the piece's condition and location of the market. While one must make their own decisions, we can offer a guide. Copyright © 1990 by Schiffer Publishing, Ltd., 1469 Morstein Road, West Chester, PA 19380, U.S.A.

Page		Piece	Price
1		sofa	600
8		armchair	550
11	A	loveseat	850
	B	end table	400
		lamp	300
	C	sewing basket	350
14	A	armchair	550
	B	armchair	550
		table	300
	C	armchair	600 set
		ottoman	
15		photographer's bench	650
16	A	settee	650
		armchair	500
	B	music stand	300
	C	table	450
18	A	rocker	650
	B	rocker	450
	C	armchair	750
19	A	chaise	850
	B	baby carriage	750
	C	high chair	450
20	A	umbrella basket	300
	B	dressing stand	1200
21	A	photographer's chair	900
	B + C	posing chair	650
22		etagere	1300
24	A	rocker	375
	B	rocker	375
25	A	rocker	450
		table	350
		table lamp	175
		armchair	500
	B	rocker	200
26	A	recamier	800
		tray	150
	B	photographer's chair	450
27	A	armchair	400
	B	armchair	550
28	A	platform rocker	550
		floor lamp	600
	B	couch	450
30	B	armchair	400
32	A	Victrola	1200
	B	baby carriage	400
33	A	twins carriage	800
	B	baby coach	1000
		baby carriage	500
34	A	child's rocker	200
	B	baby carriage	400
35	A	chaise lounge	900
	B	dining room table	800
		chairs	1600 set
36	A	lectern	350
	B	floor lamp	750
37	A	sofa	700
	B	sofa	1400 set
		armchair	
38	A	rocker	400
		armchair	400
	B	sofa	700
39	A	table	250
		left armchair	400
		right armchair	350
	B	rocker	350
		armchair	350
41	A	platform rocker	600
		table	350
	B	desk	550
		chair	250
45	B	planter	450
47		chair	900
49		armchair	1175
		sofa	1975
53	A	piano stool	400
	B	music stand	350
54	A	corner whatnot	1200
	B	platform rocker	450
55	A	whatnot	850
	B	armchair	500
56		rocker	450
57	A	floor lamp	750
	B	rocker	600
58	A	rocker	1000
		ottoman	300
	B	photographer's bench	700
	C	coat rack	300
59	A	rocker	550 each, 1700 for set
		armchair	
	B	Morris chair	1100
63		sofa	2079
65		baker's rack	1200
66	A	side chair	350
		sewing basket	450
	B	side chair	400
		sewing basket	550
		rocker	350
	C	sewing basket	300
		side chair	350
67	A	side chair	450
		smoking stand	150
		sewing table	350
	B	rocker	400
		table	250
68	A	armchair	450
	B	side chair	350
	C	armchair	800
69	A	tea cart	550
		settee	650
		photographer's chair	550
	B	corner chair	500
		table	450
		side chair	350
	C	armchair	650
		tea cart	550
70	A	planter	300
		armchair	350
		rocker	650
	B	table	200
		armchair	450
	C	armchair	450
		table	400
71	A	armchair	450
		table	350
	B	Morris chair frame	900
	C	chair	400
72	A	left armchair	450
		end table	300
		right armchair	350
	B	armchair	450
		table	550
		table lamp	250
	C	rocker	400
		table	200
		armchair	400
73	A	side chair	450
		towel rack	200
		corner chair	200
	B	magazine rack	200
		rocker	450
		sewing basket	450
	C	side chair	150
		table	150
74	A	armchair	300
		rocker	300
	B	rocker	275
		armchair	275
	C	table	250
		armchair	350
75	A	sewing box/seat	175
		desk	350
		chair	175
	B	armchair	300
		rocker	300
	C	armchair	350
		desk	500
76	A	chair	450
		floor lamp	650
		sewing table	200
	B	armchair	350
		desk	550
77	A	left armchair	250
		right armchair	400
	B	table	250
		rocker	400
		table lamp	75
	C	chest	600
		armchair	200
		end table	200
78	A	rocker	350
		plant stand	400
		rocker	250
	B	armchair	350
79	A	left armchair	300
		rocker	350
		right armchair	250
	B	rocker	300
		table	450

	armchair	300	
C	left armchair	300	
	table	250	
	right armchair	500	
A	armchair	350	
	center planter	100	
	right planter	150	
B	armchair	350	
	rocker	350	
A	table	300	
	armchair	300	
	planter	175	
B	rocker	450	
	table	300	
	armchair	450	
C	rocker	350	
	table	350	
	armchair	350	
A	side chair	250	
	armchair	350	
B	rocker	350	
	log carrier	100	
	armchair	250	
A	side chair	200	
	desk	500	
B	desk	450	set
	chair		
	floor lamp	400	
C	armchair	300	
	table	150	
A	armchair	700	set
	ottoman		
B	fernery	95	
	desk	650	set
	chair		
C	desk	300	set
	chair		
	table lamp	150	
A	armchair	600	
	table	200	
	table lamp	200	
B	left armchair	350	
	right armchair	400	
A	rocker	450	
B	platform rocker	650	
	rocker	450	
C	rocker	400	
A	platform rocker	550	
	baby's dressing stand	150	
B	rocker	500	
A	table	300	
	magazine rack	350	
	rocker	350	
B	left rocker	350	
	armchair	350	
	right rocker	350	
A	rocker	500	
	plant stand	400	
	platform rocker	650	
B	rocker	550	
C	rocker	400	
A	rocker	500	
B	platform rocker	650	
	sewing stand	200	

	C	left rocker	400
		center rocker	350
		right rocker	300
91	A	table	450
		table lamp	200
		rocker	450
	B	floor lamp	450
		rocker	400
	C	table	250
		rocker	350
92	A	Turkish bench	550
	B	wheelchair	500
	C	wheelchair	450
93	A	photographer's bench	750
	B	Turkish bench	650
	C	Turkish bench	650
94	A	armchair	350
		child's rocker	350
		rocker	500
	B	left rocker	250
		right rocker	350
	C	left rocker	250
		right rocker	175
95	A	rocker	250
		grocery cart	250
	B	rocker	350
	C	cabana chair	600
96	A	left rocker	300
		center rocker	300
		armchair	250
	B	rocker	350
		sewing box	200
	C	sewing table	200
		rocker	300
97	A	wheelchair	350
	B	rocker	400
		plant stand	300
		table	200
	C	rocker	300
98	A	left rocker	275
		stand	450
		right rocker	400
	B	table	200
		rocker	250
		sewing basket	200
99	A	table	300
		table lamp	250
		settee	750
	B	smoking stand	200
		settee	700
		table	500
		table lamp	250
100	A	settee	750
		table	250
		table lamp	250
	B	chair	400
		loveseat	600
101	A	tea cart	550
		settee	550
	B	loveseat	800
	C	settee	500
102	A	table	300
		loveseat	550
	B	sofa	600

103	A	loveseat	550
	B	sofa	700
104	A	armchair	250
		sofa	500
	B	sofa	500
		table	150
105	A	sofa	550
		tea cart	650
	B	armchair	350
		settee	650
	C	sofa	600
		child's chair	200
106	A	sofa	650
	B	sofa	650
	C	sofa	700
107	A	sofa	700
	B	sofa	550
	C	loveseat	450
108	A	sofa	650
	B	sofa	600
		armchair	300
	C	sofa	500
109	A	sofa	550
		armchair	250
	B	rocker	250
		sofa	550
	C	armchair	350
		shelves	400
		settee	500
110	A	lounge	650
	B	deck chair	700
111	A	floor lamp	600
		lounge	650
	B + C	fainting couch	800
112	A	table	200
		chaise lounge	750
		plant stand	200
	B	end table	250
		lounge	500
	C	chaise lounge	700
113	A	lounge chair	850
	B	bed	1500
		left lamp	250
		right lamp	300
114	A	lounge	650
		floor lamp	550
	B	lounge chair	600
	C	daybed	650
115	A	table	300
		lounge chair	650
	B	lounge chair	500
116		dining room table	600
		reception chairs	400 each
		corner whatnot	300
117		plant stand	300
		taller plant stand	300
		tea cart	550
		armchairs	800 each
		settee	1100
		rocker	600
		heart basket	250
		table	350
		ottoman	250
118	A	armchair	350

		rocker	350
	B	sofa	800, 1600 set
119	A	armchair	300
		table	200
		rocker	300
	B	sofa	500, 1200 set
120	A	sofa	700, 2150 set
B		rocker	400
		armchair	400
		table	450
121	A	armchair	400
		floor lamp	400
		rocker	400
	B	sofa	800, 1600 set
122	A	left armchair	300
		right armchair	300
	B	sofa	600, 1600 set
		table	400
123	A	armchair	250
	B	sofa	650
124	A	floor lamp	700
		sofa	950, 2000 set
	B	armchair	350
		table	350
		rocker	350
126	A	floor lamp	400
		table	750
		table lamp	250
	B	table	400
127	A	table	600
	B	table	700
	C	table	650
128	A	stand	450
	B	desk	550
		table lamp	250
	C	end table	300
		planter	300
129	A	armchair	250
		table	300
	B	table	500
	C	buffet table	350
130	A	left table	300
		right table	250
	B	armchair	350
		table	250
	C	telephone stand	250
		stool	150
131	A	table	300
		planter	550
	B	library table	350
	C	desk	450
		table lamp	250
132	A	sewing table	350
	B	table	200
	C	table	350
133	A	table	400
		table lamp	200
	B	table	350
		loveseat	250
	C	table	250
134	A + C	infant stroller	550
	B	infant stroller	800
135	A	baby carriage	850
	B	baby carriage	700

136	A	junior chair	400
	B	doll's swing cradle	450
	C	baby swing cradle	1000
	D	junior chair	400
137	A	child's rocker	450
	B	child's chair	300
	C	child's rocker	400
138	A	laundry hamper	250
		commode	200
		rocker	250
	B	child's washstand	250
	C	baby's dressing stand	200
139	A	bassinet	400
	B	high chair	250
	C	crib	750
140	A	left dining chair	95
		center dining chair	95
		baby's dressing stand	150
	B	rocking crib	800
141	A	crib	800
	B	bassinet	500
	C	serving stand	450
142	A	child's armchair	200
		baby scale	100
		basket	75
	B	baby carriage	200
	C	crib	650
143	A	fretwork	550
	B	Turkish bench	550
	C	fire screen	550
	D	floor lamp	650
144	A	flower baskets	100 each
		fire screen	300
	B	fire screen	450
	C	whatnot	350
145	A	easel	450
		picture frame	600
	B	whatnot	350
	C	whatnot	350
146	A	planter	700
	B	shelf	350
	C	desk	700
147	A	hat rack	450
		log carrier	200
		chair	350
	B + C	Victrola	1295
148	A	grandfather clock case	550
	B	floor lamp	450
	C	lingerie chest	650
149	A	corner clock etagere	850
	B + C	Victrola	1500
150	A	desk/table	450
		coat rack	300
	B	dresser	700
151	A	tea cart	600
	B	planter	450
	C	plant stand	175
		tea cart	350
	D	tea cart	350
back cover		chairs	400 each
		table	600